FAN THE DECK

An Advanced Composition Book

Robert B. Cahill and Herbert J. Hrebic

Contributions

James Hanna
Dianne Johnson
Marguerite Munk

Edited by

Theresa Zigmond

Acknowledgments

We would like to thank the following students for allowing us to use their papers as samples: Joseph Browne, Kenneth Bruhns, Charles Couper, Daniel Flens, Joseph Florek, James Kaphusman, Mary Lenehan, Raymond Kennelly, Keith Kostecka, Leanne Michener, Richard Muszynski, Daniel Nalezny, Mary O'Malley, Staci Ness, Thomas Pyzik, Edward Suda, John VerKuilen, Derrick White, and Stephen Wonderlick.

We owe a depth of gratitude to our friends and relatives who proofread the first draft and offered sound advice in helping us revise *Fan the Deck*: Mary Jane Cahill, Diane Franchini, Maureen Lighthall, Catherine Morrin, Bob Lyon, Marguerite Munk, Hank Schwieterman, Jean Searls, and Ginger Zigmond.

We are grateful for the topics in the **writing across the curriculum** selection in each composition unit from a number of dedicated educators: Reverend William Corcoran, Heather Hopkins, Andy Montelone, Dr. Myles Phipps, Ralph Rzeszutko, and especially Diane Kozojed for coordinating our efforts in developing the various topics.

We would like to thank Jim Hanna and Dianne Johnson, who submitted the **Problem-Solution Report** as a class project in one of our graduate writing classes and allowed us to adapt their project in *Fan*, and Marguerite Munk, who wrote the **College Application Letter** unit and field-tested it with her students.

Finally, we owe a special thank you to Theresa Zigmond who spent tedious hours editing *Fan the Deck* and demonstrated the patience of a saint in working with the shorter half of the Booboo-Yogi team. Without Theresa's persistence and effort, we would not have finished the revised edition on schedule.

ISBN 0-933282-27-3 paperback
ISBN 0-933282-28-1 hard cover

Table of Contents

To all our friends

who helped with this revised edition.

h

A **definition paper** is a popular assignment in College Freshmen English. We begin *Fan the Deck* with this writing assignment for two reasons. First, writing a **definition paper** will train you to think in a systematic order. You will be required to select an abstract word or phrase, funnel it down to its narrowest classification, brainstorm supportive ideas, and organize your ideas in a logical sequence. In short, you will practice a writing process that you will use every time you are assigned a composition, whether in a social studies class, a science class, or an English class.

Second, we want to prepare you for the day that you walk into your first college composition class, whether in some Ivy League school or in a junior college, and Professor Stoneface assigns you a **definition paper**. We want you to feel confident because you had written one in high school.
We want you to *ace* that assignment.

STAGE ONE: PREWRITING

STUDENT LEARNING OBJECTIVES

1. The student will select an abstract word or phrase as the subject for a definition paper.
2. The student will define her term by first mentioning the class or *genus* and then by funneling down the term to its narrowest classification.
3. The student will explain the unique characteristics of her term which make it special and different from other *objects* in the same class.
4. The student will explain the term in depth by using a variety of methods of defining.
5. The student will organize her ideas in a logical sequence, demonstrating orderly thinking.

HELPFUL DRILLS

As a good communicator, you must select words carefully so that your listener or reader understands what you are saying or writing. The meanings of your words must be clear. An important skill for you to acquire, therefore, is the ability to write clear definitions.

There are many strategies that can be used to write a **definition paper**. Before you select an abstract word or phrase as your topic, review and learn these various methods of defining. Afterwards you will have to determine which of these techniques will aid you in writing a comprehensive definition that your audience will understand.

Here are the **seven methods** of defining a word or phrase:

1. FORMAL DEFINITION

Probably the most popular method used in definition papers is the formal definition of the term. The writer simply states the class or *genus* of a term, and then provides specific ways in which the term differs from other terms within the same class. Here are some examples:

Word	Class (*Genus*)	Distinguishing Characteristics
Argumentative prose is a	type of writing	which provides logical reasons to convince someone of the writer's opinion on a specific topic.
A calculator is an	electronic device	that performs arithmetical processes.
A bicycle is a	two-wheeled vehicle	driven by pedals and used as a means of transportation.

As the writer develops his definition, he will expand on the meaning of the word by using some of the other methods to define the term. He might support the formal definition with illustrations or examples or possibly explain some of the key functions of the term.

Mistakes in Formal Definitions

In writing formal definitions, inexperienced writers often make the class or *genus* too general, too broad, too all encompassing. For example, in defining a *whale*, one student wrote:

A whale is a large sea creature, which is hunted for its oil and flesh.

The class *large sea creature* is too broad. A shark or a squid or a manta ray is also a *large sea creature.*

2

The student needed to funnel down the class or *genus* further. Here is his revised definition:

A whale is a *large aquatic mammal* that breathes air but cannot survive . . .

What about defining the object *spoon*? What would be wrong if you used the term *household device* to explain the class or *genus* of a spoon? Here is a definition of *spoon*:

A *spoon* is a kitchen utensil, consisting of an oval or round small bowl and a handle used for conveying food to the mouth or for stirring or measuring.

Better!

Repeating the word or a form of the word is another mistake in writing formal definitions. You do not want to define *a critic* as a person who *criticizes*. The purpose of writing a definition is to explain the precise meaning of a word, not to write in circles, repeating the same words.

In writing a formal definition, you should also avoid the expressions *is when* or *is where*. For example, *criticism is when* a *critic criticizes* bad things in a movie or play. What is a better definition of *criticism*?

EXERCISE 1: Write formal definitions for some of the following writing across the curriculum terms. Each definition must include the class or genus funneled down to its narrowest classification and the unique characteristics of the term. Define two or three of the terms as a class activity before writing formal definitions for some of the other terms.

physical education	**social studies**	**science**	**shop**
basketball	map	Bunsen burner	goggles
parallel bars	encyclopedia	beaker	apron
locker	globe	microscope	hammer

home economics	**foreign language**	**math**	**English**
microwave oven	chapeau (French)	protractor	notebook
spatula	pinata (Spanish)	polygon	folder
food processor	tape recorder	eraser	dictionary

EXERCISE 2: Rewrite the following formal definitions and be prepared to share your responses. Remember each class or *genus* should be funneled down to its narrowest classification. Avoid *is when* or *is where* expressions, and also avoid repeating a form of the word in the definition.

1. Prejudice is when a person dislikes another person without good reasons.
2. Narrative writing is where a writer narrates a story in chronological sequence.
3. Hockey is a game in which two teams try to get an object into the opponent's goal.
4. Love is when you never have to say you are sorry.
5. A computer is a machine which computes information.

2. EXAMPLES OR ILLUSTRATIONS

Another method for defining a word is the use of examples or illustrations that the reader can understand. The example or illustration is a fact which the reader can identify with and relate to. In using examples or illustrations, the writer makes a generalization clearer, more interesting, and more convincing than the term would be by itself. The abstract becomes concrete.

For example, teachers and coaches often speak of students' demonstrating their *pride* in their school in everything they do. What is *school pride*?

In writing the formal definition of the phrase *school pride*, one might say that it is a *feeling of loyalty and satisfaction which enables a student to feel good about his school.* To make the phrase *school pride* more meaningful for the reader, however, the writer would probably need to expand with specific examples and illustrations that demonstrate *school pride* in action.

For instance, how about a student's returning a messed-up food tray at the end of the last lunch period without anyone seeing him do this? Or cheering wildly at a volleyball game when your school has lost the first set 15-1 and trails the second game 14-0 with your opponent serving? Or staying up all night to decorate the gym for the winter carnival despite having a math test at 8:15 the next morning? These are all examples of *school pride*. Can you think of others?

EXERCISE 3: Discuss examples and illustrations to define the following terms.

1. The term *class* is often used to describe people. Select specific individuals who demonstrate *class*, and provide specific examples and illustrations to support your definition.
2. The term *tough love* is often used in explaining the relationship between parents and their children. Provide specific examples and illustrations of *tough love* on the part of parents.
3. Provide specific examples and illustrations of *true friendship* among teenagers.

3. FUNCTIONAL DEFINITION

Similar to examples and illustrations as a method of defining a term, a functional definition shows what a term is by how it works. The writer directly states what something is and then shows how it functions. This method of defining provides the reader with a checklist to test whether or not the term does what it is supposed to do.

In addition, this method is an objective way of defining a word in a simple yet practical way. It is especially useful in defining abstract terms. For example, "Freedom of speech is a liberty given to all Americans." This definition is too subjective, not specific enough. The functional definition might sound something like this: "Freedom of speech is a liberty granted to all American citizens which allows us to disagree with our country's policies without fear of imprisonment." You could go on to explain other functions of freedom of speech.

If you were writing a definition paper in which you were defining what a good mother is, you might define her by explaining some of her roles or functions.

A good mother is a *worrier*, a person who, despite working eight hours at the office or the factory, sits up in the living room until 3:30 A.M. for her teenager who missed the 12:30 A.M. curfew.

A good mother is a *jack of all trades.* She can fix the flat tire on the bicycle, tape the old baseball with Curad's adhesive tape for the afternoon game, bandage the scraped knee from the skateboard fall, or clean the mess from the parrot who escaped from the cage and knocked over dad's pipe rack.

EXERCISE 4: Write functional definitions for the following terms. Practice one or two of these as a group activity before working on your own.

1. *Success* in high school.
2. What makes a *good teacher?*
3. *Fun* at a three-year-old's party.
4. *Democracy* in student government.
5. High school *reunions.*

4 . NEGATION

Sometimes it is easier for the reader to understand a term if he knows what the term is **not**. In other words, the writer supplies a series of negative statements, specifically stating what the term does **not** mean or do.

Negative definitions are especially helpful in defining abstract terms. They enable the writer to pinpoint his definition by suggesting ideas the reader should **not** consider the term to mean. For example, in defining *freedom of the press,* a student wrote the following:

> Freedom of the press does **not** entitle reporters to dig into a citizen's private life and print everything they discover about the individual. It does **not** allow them to slant their stories so that they can create sensationalism to make a name for themselves and increase their newspaper's circulation. It does **not** allow a TV journalist the right to renege on a previous agreement and question . . .

EXERCISE 5: Use the same terms from **EXERCISE 3** on page 4. Discuss different negative statements that you could use to show what *class*, *tough love*, and *true friendship* are **not**.

5 . COMPARISON

A simile is a figure of speech using the words *like* or *as* to compare two unlike things. The writer will select an object that is essentially unlike the term being defined except for one resemblance. This resemblance is normally something that the reader can easily understand.

> Bigotry is *like* a festering wound, oozing out poisons that destroy the body.

> Love is *like* a sweet, red rose, freshly plucked from the spring garden after a gentle rain.

If you use a simile in defining your term, you must be aware that comparisons are not perfect. They are close to, parallel, alike, linked, correlated, analogous, similar, but not equal. Therefore, in order to define your term completely, you must use additional methods of definition in your composition.

EXERCISE 6: Write comparisons for the following words using *like* or *as*.

1. Marriage	**3.** Pessimism	**5.** Success	**7.** Detention
2. Mischievous	**4.** Death	**6.** Suspension	**8.** Exhilaration

Marriage is *like* . . .

6. SYNONYMS

Another way of defining a word is by giving synonyms for the word, that is, providing words or phrases with a meaning similar to the word being defined. Like the comparison method, however, each synonym is slightly different in meaning from the selected word. It is not exact. Although synonyms help your reader receive a better understanding of your selected word, do not rely exclusively on them in providing a complete definition. They should be used in combination with the other methods. Here are some examples of synonyms:

Church: house of God, temple, place of worship, holy place, shrine, basilica, mosque, synagogue, sanctuary, meeting place.

Brave: daring, valiant, intrepid, chivalrous, valorous, heroic, gallant, undaunted, indomitable, spunky, resolute, firm.

Optimism: confidence, assurance, good cheer, upbeat, cheerfulness, enthusiasm, elation, hopefulness, exuberance.

EXERCISE 7: Provide synonyms for the following words. Brainstorm your own ideas before looking up the words in a thesaurus.

1. Policeman	**5.** Naive
2. Said	**6.** Happiness
3. Hopelessness	**7.** Geek
4. Obscene	**8.** Noble

7. TRACING THE HISTORY OR EVOLUTION OF THE WORD

A final method of defining a word is tracing its history or evolution. Obviously, this would require research since you need to discover where the term originated and how it has developed and possibly changed meaning(s) over the years. This could be very interesting and worthwhile information for your reader to know.

EXERCISE 8: Review: As a class activity, read the following student definition paper. Then discuss which methods of defining were used.

Maelstrom: The Waves of Chaos

(A) The English language is one which has many colorful and descriptive words, both of English origin and borrowed from other tongues. However, many of these words are not widely used because people are unaccustomed to hearing them. One of these words is *maelstrom*. But what really is a *maelstrom*?

(B) It is defined as a large, destructive current or whirlpool, specifically, one off the coast of Scandinavia, and the word is originally from there. There are, though, other meanings. The implications of the word are chaos and violence. In fact, the second abstract definition is a great destructive force or a confused or turbulent state of mind, emotion or affairs.

(C) Consider the very sound of the word. Say it aloud. It even sounds violent, but also mysterious at once.

(D) Here are other examples of the word in use. "An accumulated mass, in one wild *maelstrom* of affrighted men, struggling in frantic eddies," wrote J. S. C. Abbot about a battle, which is both greatly violent and greatly confused. In 1850 Miss Braddon wrote, "Every gutter in every one of these streets was a little Niagara, with a *maelstrom* at the corner." This sentence is quite interesting because it refers to both the literal and figurative definitions. It refers both to the storm-sewers and the great activity occurring on the street.

(E) A beehive is "a *maelstrom* of activity," because the bees all seem to be coming and going at will about the hive, though it really is quite an organized place. A good example from history is World War I. The effects caused the downfall of the old orders left over from centuries back, directly leading to the confusion of the 20's, depression of the 30's, and war again in the 40's.

(F) A *maelstrom* is like a raging blaze in a turbulent wind. Its destruction is meted out in random directions; it can become uncontrollable in a moment.

(G) Overall, a *maelstrom* seems very elemental in its violence and destruction. The word has an interesting history, and would make a good addition to anyone's vocabulary.

WRITING PROMPTS

You will be given three choices in writing a **definition paper**. Select the one that enables you to define your term as completely as possible.

1. Abstract Word: You are an etymologist, an expert in the origin and development of words. In order to prove your expertise, you must select an abstract word or phrase and define it using the methods described in the **Helpful Drills**.

When your definition assignment is finished, your reader will know that you understand your term thoroughly, having taken into account all the characteristics of your term. In fact, your definition will be so complete that there will be no doubt as to the exact meaning of your term.

Besides the suggested abstract words that follow, you might want to examine a vocabulary workbook for a term/word that interests you more. The student who defined *maelstrom* found that word in his vocabulary workbook.

a. Honor	**f.** Conscience	**k.** Feminine	**p.** Morality
b. Nostalgia	**g.** Sportsmanship	**l.** Evil	**q.** Hero
c. Dilemma	**h.** Failure	**m.** Heaven	**r.** Freedom
d. Workaholic	**i.** Conceit	**n.** Peace	**s.** Duty
e. Service	**j.** Peer pressure	**o.** Apathy	**t.** Horror

2. Writing Across the Curriculum: As often as we can in *Fan the Deck*, we will suggest your selecting a topic for each writing assignment from one of your other academic classes. This serves two purposes. First, it emphasizes that the skills taught in *Fan* should be reinforced every time you write a composition, not only in an English class.

Second, it might help you learn more about a topic from another content area. When you are given choices for selecting a topic in *this* class, ask your social studies teacher, science teacher, math teacher, computer teacher, etc., for possible topics that fit into the type of paper being taught. For this composition, you will need an abstract word or phrase to define.

Here are some examples:

Literature	Social Studies	Chemistry	Physics
1. Puritan ethic	1. Checks and Balances	1. Compound	1. Space
2. Renaissance man	2. Civil Disobedience	2. Reaction	2. Electricity
3. Tragic hero	3. Cold War	3. State	3. Energy
4. Realism	4, Capitalism	4. Motion	4. Atom
5. Romanticism	5. Laissez-faire	5. Matter	5. Theory

Mathematics	Foreign Language	P. E. /Sports	Biology
1. Parallel	1. Culture	1. Hustle	1. Osmosis
2. Tangent	2. Coup d'état	2. Teamwork	2. Motion
3. Parabola	3. Folklore	3. Heart	3. Genetics
4. Equation	4. Humanities	4. Rhubarb	4. Life
5. Probability	5. Linguistics	5. A Winner	5. Habitat

3. Essay Writing Contest: Quite frequently local businesses or special interest groups, like the American Legion, Rotary Club, and The Daughters of the American Revolution sponsor essay writing contests to commemorate an historic event.

Your third option for this assignment, then, is to check your school bulletin boards or talk with your guidance counselors to find out if any groups are sponsoring an essay writing contest dealing with a definition. You will not only have an excellent topic for this assignment, but also may have a chance to win mega bucks to use as a down payment on that '57 Chevy or to put toward your first semester college tuition.

Now you must decide which abstract word or phrase to define based on your three choices. No two students may select the same word. If a dispute arises, possibly a lottery could be held. Instead of winning $10,000,000, however, the winner gets the word of her choice. As you begin to think of terms to consider, reflect on these questions:

1. What abstract word or phrase do I know or want to know more about?
2. Will I have to do some research on my term, regarding its history or evolution?
3. Can I think of an abstract word from another content area?
4. As I brainstorm, am I considering all the characteristics of the term?

PURPOSE AND AUDIENCE

Once you have selected an abstract word or phrase to define, you should decide on your purpose. Since this is a definition paper, your purpose will be to define your term as completely as possible so that your reader will understand your word as thoroughly as you do. Knowing what you want to achieve will help you concentrate on your content and the organization of your ideas.

Since the main purpose of writing is to communicate ideas, it is important that you know with whom you are communicating every time you write. In other words, you must know your audience.

Knowing your audience will help determine the words that you will use and also the supportive ideas necessary to achieve your purpose. For example, if you were writing a **definition paper** to a six-year-old, you would have to be selective in your vocabulary and specific examples. You would need to use both words and examples that the six-year-old could understand. Determining your audience, then, is necessary in writing a good composition.

For this assignment your audience is your classmates. Assume they know absolutely nothing about your term. Since you are the expert, your goal is to make them experts.

THINK SHEET

A **Think Sheet** is the part of the prewriting stage where the writer thinks with pen in hand. It is the time to gather thoughts into a list of ideas that will be included into the first draft. If you can make a list with very specific details, you will have little trouble with your paper's content.

If you cannot make an adequate list, you probably are trying to write a paper for which you do not have enough information. If this is the case, you will avoid frustrations by perhaps selecting a new abstract term or do a little more research. It is okay to start over. You will have proved the usefulness of the **Think Sheet**.

For this definition paper we have designed a special **Think Sheet** based on the various methods used to define a word that you have studied in the **Helpful Drill** section of this unit.

EXERCISE 9: Before you begin to complete your own **Think Sheet**, complete a group **Think Sheet** for one of the words in subject selection choice number 1, page 9, using the **Think Sheet** on pages 13-14. Although each method for defining a word might not be appropriate for each term, try to come up with ideas for each category when you are completing the group **Think Sheet**.

Practice!

Now that you have practiced a group **Think Sheet**, fill out your own **Think Sheet**. One way to do this is to sit down and talk your abstract word or phrase through with a fellow student, a friend, a parent, Cousin Wally, anybody you can find to be your listener. Let them ask questions. You might even record your conversation to help you recall the ideas as you are jotting them down on the **Think Sheet**. Talking it over will help you when you begin to write your first draft.

As you begin to fill out your individual **Think Sheet**, try to list ideas for each method of definition even though some of them might not be appropriate for your specific word. You can always subtract the unnecessary ideas as you begin to write your first draft.

After you complete your **Think Sheet**, show it to your teacher. She will tell you if you have enough material to begin writing. She might even ask you to share your **Think Sheet** with the class for group discussion, or she may have you exchange your **Think Sheet** with a classmate for peer analysis.

Definition Paper Think Sheet

1. Write the abstract word or phrase being defined._____

2. Write the formal definition of the word, including its class or *genus*, and its distinguishing characteristics.

_____

_____

_____

_____

_____

3. List specific examples or illustrations of the word or phrase.

a. _____

b. _____

c. _____

d. _____

e. _____

f. _____

4. List "functions" of the word or phrase: what it does or how it works.

a. _____

b. _____

c. _____

d. _____

e. _____

f. _____

5. List ideas your abstract word or phrase is **not**. (Negation)

a. _____

b. _____

c. _____

d. _____

e. _____

f. _____

6. Write some comparisons of the word or phrase using *like* or *as*.

a. _____

b. _____

c. _____

7.   Write some synonyms for your word or phrase.

_____

_____

_____

8. Trace the history or evolution of the word.

_____

_____

_____

_____

9. Write a sentence which states your paper's purpose.

_____

_____

_____

STAGE TWO: WRITING THE FIRST DRAFT

With your completed **Think Sheet** in front of you, write your first draft as quickly as possible. If you think of additional ideas that are not included on your **Think Sheet**, write them on your first draft as long as they support your purpose. Think of your audience as you are writing.

Do not worry about punctuation, capitalization, spelling, sentence variety, etc., at this time. You can correct those errors when you revise your composition. Also, write on every other line and number each sentence.

ORGANIZING THE PAPER

Your main purpose in this assignment is to define a word or phrase so completely that your reader shares in your expertise. Consequently, you are not being told to write a specific number of words, for example, a 500 or 1,000 word composition. Instead, you must define your word or phrase so **completely** that your audience knows you are an expert on that term even if it requires 749 words or 1, 346 words. One hundred and fifty will not do!

Before you write your first draft, look over the specific ideas and methods you brainstormed on your **Think Sheet** and select the ones that help prove your knowledge on your word or phrase. Organize them in a logical sequence that will demonstrate orderly thinking on your part. For example, if you analyze the organization of the **Maelstrom: Waves of Chaos** student composition on page 8, note how the student structured his composition:

1. His opening paragraph mentioned that many colorful and descriptive words in English are borrowed from other languages but are not commonly used because most people are unaware of them. He then stated *maelstrom* is one such word, and used a question as his controlling idea or thesis.
2. His first and second developmental paragraphs presented a **formal definition**, and also offered a **brief history** and **description** of the word.
3. His third developmental paragraph provided **examples** of the word in use. He even quotes from a reliable source.
4. His fourth developmental paragraph offered a **comparison**.
5. He concluded his composition by presenting his opinion of the word, suggesting that it would make a "good addition to one's vocabulary."

At this time do not be concerned with writing a specific type of introductory paragraph. Sometimes it is much easier to write an effective introductory paragraph **after** you know what you are going to introduce.

Later on in this unit we will present different types of introductory paragraphs.

Here are some things to consider in writing your first draft:

1. If you include a formal definition, make sure you funnel down the class or *genus* to its narrowest classification.
2. Use as many methods of defining as are needed to provide a complete explanation of your term.
3. With each method used, be specific with your ideas. Use examples, functions, negations, comparisons, and synonyms, etc., that your audience can understand.
4. Organize your methods in a sequence that demonstrates orderly thinking.

COHERENCE (GLUING TOGETHER IDEAS)

The organization of your developmental paragraphs will help carry your reader from one thought to the next. When you wrote a story in junior high school or freshmen English, you told the events in a chronological sequence. Since this sequence is a natural time order, the paragraphs were easy for your reader to follow. However, in writing a **definition paper**, the order is not so obvious. It is important, then, that you make the relationship of ideas clear. Transition words can help achieve this.

Here are some transition words that might prove helpful:

Transition Words: first, second, next, yet, finally, on the other hand, etc.

Another means of linking paragraphs is to use topic sentences as transitions. Topic sentences serve two purposes: first, they introduce the subject of their paragraph; second, they link the new paragraph with the preceding one.

Now write your first draft.

INTRODUCTORY PARAGRAPHS

Writing an introductory paragraph is one of the most difficult parts in writing a composition. Since the purposes of an introductory paragraph are to capture your reader's interest and to introduce your subject, you want to spend some time planning an effective opening. That is why we suggested that you concentrate on a specific type of introductory paragraph **after** you have written the body of your paper or at least planned on the content. It is easier to write an introduction once you know what you are going to introduce.

Here are some specific types of introductions that might be appropriate for a **definition paper**:

Definition Introductory Paragraph

Probably the most standard way of opening a **definition paper** is to begin with the formal definition of the word. You simply state the class or *genus* of the term, and provide specific characteristics showing how your term is different from other objects in the same class.

Negation Introductory Paragraph

Not only is **negation** a specific method of defining a word or phrase, but it is also an effective opening. You can begin your introduction by explaining what your word is **not**. Your last sentence in your introduction might be a formal definition, specifically defining your word in positive terms.

Question Introductory Paragraph

A question or series of questions is also an effective way to begin a composition, especially if you are going to answer the question(s) in the body of your composition. In the **Maelstrom: Wave of Chaos** model, the student ended up with a question as his controlling idea. The remainder of the composition answered the question: "What is a maelstrom?"

Incident Introductory Paragraph

Many students begin their compositions by narrating an incident that is relevant to their topic. They simply tell how the idea for their assignment came about in a story form before writing their controlling idea.

CONCLUDING PARAGRAPH

Since your conclusion is the last idea your reader will read, you need to spend time thinking about an effective way to end your composition. Like an introductory paragraph, a conclusion has two purposes. First, the reader should understand your paper's purpose. Second, it should leave the reader with a sense of finality.

Here are two types of conclusion that might be appropriate for a **definition paper**:

Significance of Term Concluding Paragraph

This type of ending is effective if your purpose is to let your reader know why it is important to understand your specific term. He discovers the significance of your abstract word or phrase.

Restating the Controlling Idea Concluding Paragraph

Probably the most common type of ending is a statement which restates the controlling idea of the introductory paragraph in different words.

STAGE THREE: REWRITING

SENTENCE OPENING SHEET

After you have written your first draft including your introductory and concluding paragraphs, fill out the **Sentence Opening Sheet**. If you have used either *Cut the Deck* or *Stack the Deck*, you are familiar with this step in the rewriting stage. The **SOS** sheet can help you diagnose your paper's strengths and weaknesses at a glance once you learn how to use it.

For longer compositions, it is not necessary to complete a **Sentence Opening Sheet** for every paragraph unless directed by your teacher. Instead, select one or two paragraphs to analyze using the **SOS** sheet format. Once you identify your strengths and weaknesses for the selected paragraphs, you will know what to look for in the remainder of the composition.

When you begin to analyze your paper without needing the **SOS** sheet, you can eliminate this step in the writing process. We do not want to kill the skill with overdrill. On the bottom of the **SOS** sheet you should indicate the revisions you want to make on the first draft. These comments are your personal contract.

Your **Sentence Opening Sheet** should include the following information:

Column One
Variety/Fragments

Write in the **first four words** of each sentence.

1 . Check to see if your sentences begin with the same structures. Avoid weak and unemphatic openers such as *there is, there are, I think*, and *in my opinion.* Vary your openings. (**VAR** stands for variety.)

2 . Check to see if too many of your sentences begin with *the* or with the subject or subject-verb pattern. You should **combine** this sentence with the next one or **rearrange** ideas by emphasizing a different sentence element at the beginning.

Examples:

One needs to understand all the facts **before answering the question.**
Before answering the question, one needs to understand all the facts.

Wilma spoke of her past **reluctantly.**
Reluctantly, Wilma spoke of her past.

I do not understand **that question.**
That question I do not understand.

Carlton sank the three point shot **as the siren blared ending the game.**
As the siren blared ending the game, Carlton sank the three point shot.

The Zigmond family **was blinded by the blizzard**, and they lost their way.
Blinded by the blizzard, the Zigmond family lost their way.

3 . If your sentences begin with subordinating conjunctions, check to see that the sentences are complete thoughts and not fragments. A comma follows the introductory clause.

Fragment: **If** we wish to remain free. We must be willing to defend our rights.

Revised: **If** we wish to remain free, we must be willing to defend our rights.

Write in the **special** words your teacher wants you to refrain from using.

These words vary for each assignment depending upon your purpose.

1. If you shift your point of view from first person to second person to third person within the same composition, your teacher might have you list the *forbidden* pronouns for the composition, e.g., "I think," "you know," etc.
2. If you use weak, general words such as *nice, stuff, thing, a lot, good, very*, etc., you can spot these words on your first draft, subtract them, and expand with more specific words.

Column Three   **Verb Power**

Write each **verb** used in your sentences.

1. If you shift from present tense to past tense within the same paragraph, you can correct the inconsistent verb tense.
2. If you use weak verbs like *got, goes, have, has, is, are, was, were,* etc., you can substitute for more specific and concrete verbs.
3. If you want to emphasize ideas by writing in active voice, eliminate all forms of "to be" on your final draft.

Column Four

Run-ons/Emphasis

Write in the **number of words** for each sentence.

1. If your sentences are the same lengths, you might need to combine and/or rearrange some of them for variety.
2. If one of your sentences is too long, you should check to see if it is a run-on.
3. If you want to emphasize an idea, you might want to write it as a short sentence for reader impact.

Name_____Period_____

Sentence Openings (first 4 words)	Special	Verbs He_____	# of Words

PEER EVALUATION USING A CHECKLIST SHEET

Peer evaluation is an effective way to improve writing skills. You will be reading a fellow student's composition dealing with the same type of assignment that you wrote. Sometimes it is easier to spot mistakes on someone else's paper before you rewrite your own first draft. In checking over your partner's assignment, focus on the stated objectives as listed on the **Student Objectives and Evaluation Sheet (SOES)**.

Do not be afraid of constructive suggestions, for "Nothing would be done at all if a woman (or man) waited until she (he) could do it so well that no one could find fault with it." What a great learning experience! Thank you, Cardinal Newman.

The **Student Objectives and Evaluation Sheet** (Grading Sheet) and the **Checklist Sheet** provide specific areas for you to concentrate on as you evaluate your fellow student's composition. Not only should you discuss your comments with your partner, but also write down areas of concern on his first draft.

FINAL COPY AFTER PEER EVALUATION

You will revise your first draft based on the comments from the **Checklist Sheet** you receive from your partner or support group and from your own self-evaluation. The **Student Objectives and Evaluation Sheet** and the **Sentence Opening Sheet** should give you a good idea of what you need to concentrate on in rewriting your paper.

Your final copy should be neat and error-free. Before you submit that "perfect copy," you will need to read your "revised" first draft aloud three or four times to check for the following:

1. Read the paper aloud to hear how it sounds. **Subtract** any ideas or expressions that sound confusing or are repeated.
2. Read the paper a second time to check for **spelling** errors. If you think a word is misspelled, put a mark by it and later look it up in the dictionary. If you are using a word processor, you will probably use the Spell Check to make sure all your words are spelled correctly. Do not be foolish enough to rely exclusively on the Spell Check. Check the words yourself. The Spell Check identifies words that are not spelled correctly. It does not identify a *wrong* word as long as that word is spelled correctly. Unfortunately, we **no** from embarrassing experiences. OOPS!

3. Read the paper a third time to check for general mechanics.

Definition Paper Checklist

Introductory Paragraph

1. What words in the introduction capture your interest?

Developmental Paragraphs

2. What methods of defining has the writer included in his organization?

3. Mark the transition words used to link the paragraphs on the first draft. If transition words are needed but missing to show the relationship of ideas, indicate this on the first draft.

Concluding Paragraph

4. What type of concluding paragraph did the writer use? How did it indicate a sense of finality?

Style

5. Which sentence openings need to be rearranged to add interest?

6. Which sentence lengths need to be varied to emphasize key ideas?

7. If there are any words that are too vague, substitute more specific ones next to the original words.

Mechanics

8. Edit your partner's paper for the following errors: fragments, run-ons, punctuation, capitalization, spelling, verb tense consistency, etc. **Be a friend!**

STAGE FOUR: PUBLISHING

Publishing gives you an opportunity to share your writing with an audience. For the definition paper, some volunteers might read their definition to the class or their cooperative learning group or give an oral presentation.

Also, this might be a perfect opportunity to create a class booklet of all the words being defined. It could be divided into specific categories, for example, abstract words, writing across the curriculum topics, etc.

Finally, you might want to include your definition paper in your writing portfolio.

The fourth column of the **Sentence Opening Sheet** makes you aware of how many words you have written in each sentence. Knowing how many words will help you revise your composition if you have included unnecessary words and ideas. Also, if all your sentences were written with approximately the same number of words, you can vary your sentence lengths.

First Four Words Per Sentence	Special	Verb	Number of Words Per Sentence
			32
			9
			23
			43
			50

You are a walking grammar. Since you were three or four years old, you have been speaking in simple sentences, carrying on meaningful conversations with a wide range of audiences: your peers, your parents, your aunts and uncles, neighbors, etc.

Nobody taught you how to do this. You were able to accomplish this feat because nature had equipped you with an amazing capacity to learn language without your ever being aware of it. You were born with an intuitive control over your language.

As you grew older, your simple sentences changed to compound sentences as you unconsciously recognized the different kinds of relationships between ideas. You started stringing together sentences with coordinating conjunctions mostly *but, or,* and the famous or infamous *and.*

Unfortunately, many students carry over these speech patterns into their writing and simply write the same monotonous simple and compound sentence patterns over and over. Their sentences always begin with *The, And Then, And so,* and *I,* etc., or they write the sixty word sentence by stringing all of their ideas with the same word, *and.* **YUK**! They offer no variety in their sentence structures or lengths.

To avoid writing the same sentence patterns and overly long sentences, a good writer must use a variety of sentence structures and lengths. How do you achieve this? By manipulating sentences, using the four basic sentence writing skills: **combining**, **rearranging**, **subtracting**, and **expanding**.

Once you have mastered these skills, an almost infinite number of sentence patterns is available to you as a writer. If you have used other books in our series, specifically *Cut the Deck* and *Stack the Deck*, you are familiar with these four terms and have hopefully incorporated them as part of your writing vocabulary.

WRITER'S VOCABULARY

You must learn to **combine** ideas so that you can write using a variety of sentence structures, making it more interesting for your audience.

You must learn to **rearrange** ideas so that you can position important ideas in key places where main ideas are emphasized. If an idea is important to you, your audience must know it.

You must learn to **subtract** unnecessary words and phrases so that you do not clutter up your writing with ideas that digress from your purpose.

You must learn to **expand** ideas so that you support your point of view with specific details.

In short, learning how to use these skills will make you a better writer. **Guaranteed**!

Since *Fan the Deck* is an advanced composition book, you will be required to manipulate sentences with a specific purpose in mind. You will also be required to defend your decisions. Functioning with these skills will not be enough.

SUBTRACTING UNNECESSARY WORDS AND IDEAS

Subtracting is the first major sentence manipulatory skill to be taught in *Fan the Deck*. When you revise your first draft, you should make sure that you have not included unnecessary words that detract from the quality of your writing. Knowing the number of words you have written in each sentence will *force* you to check to see if you possibly repeated words or ideas. Reading your sentences aloud enables you to hear repetition. Ask yourself these questions:

1. Did I repeat words or ideas in the same sentence?
2. Did I fill my sentences with unnecessary words such as *fact* and *what expressions* that can be subtracted?
3. Did I use too many words to express a simple idea?
4. Did I digress from the topic?

The examples below are filled with some unnecessary words and ideas:

Example: Elando was **quite** aware **of the fact that** Mr. Sager was upset with his behavior during the pep rally.

Revised: Elando was aware that Mr. Sager was upset with his pep-rally behavior.

Example: **All of a sudden** the rock concert **where rock singers** were giving a concert was stunned by a bolt of lightning **from the sky.**

Revised: Suddenly the rock concert was stunned by a bolt of lightning.

Example: **What I want to do** is to live in the Chicagoland area to be near my family.

Revised: I want to live in the Chicagoland area to be near my family.

Here are some expressions to avoid:

on account of the fact that	What I want to say
in spite of the fact that	All things being equal
due to the fact that	All of a sudden
Needless to say	What I mean is
This paper will prove that. . .	As I said previously
In the following three paragraphs	Relative Clauses (WH Words: which, who)
The reason	
In my opinion I think	There is or There are
In this day and age	"Come in contact with" for "meet"
Now I will explain	Well, . . .

EXERCISE 1: Rewrite each sentence by subtracting the unnecessary words.

1. In Shirley Jackson's famous short story "The Lottery," the ancient annual rite, although very old, of each family member picking a paper from a black box, was celebrated every June.

2. Single-handedly, the fireman put out the fire in the house which was burning and saved the little baby kitten, unassisted without any help from anyone.

3. In spite of the fact that Maurice knew he could gain more weight and would not start in the championship game, he kept on eating pasta all day long.

4. With my own ears I heard the eerie sounds coming from the attic, which is just above the top floor of the old house, which is ancient.

5. ~~In the body of my composition I have proven to you that~~ Creon was an unreasonable, selfish, and tyrannical ruler and ~~that~~ his actions destroyed the heroine Antigone.

6. ~~There are~~ two different software programs ~~that~~ could be used ~~in order to be of some~~ benefit to students ~~who have an occasion and the~~ *with* need to use a good word processing program.

7. What I want to say is that I would not be able to go away over the Christmas holidays due to the fact that I have to finish a research paper, which was assigned to me by my history teacher on the last day of class before Christmas.

8. In the following three paragraphs I intend to prove to you that the major theme of Upton Sinclair's *The Jungle* revolves around the idea of man's inhumanity to his fellow man as seen through the eyes of the main character of the novel, Jurgis Rudkus.

9. While Stacey was in London, she had the occasion to shop after Christmas at London's famous store, Harrods.

10. Wallace Rivers did his homework in a manner that proved he did not care to do his homework.

11. ~~The~~ seniors worked hard ~~in~~ the advanced composition course, ~~and they~~ learned a functional approach to writing, and ~~they~~ prepared ~~themselves~~ for ~~other~~ writing assignments ~~in the academic career.~~

12. Comedian Rodney Dangerfield, who tells jokes, owns his own nightclub and is famous and is also a comedian in movies.

13. Living on Lake Shore Drive, we enjoyed a view of the lake where we lived.

14. The summary section of the history book summarized the major events leading up to the Civil War in a summary format.

15. The reason that we honor Dr. Martin Luther King on January 15th is due to the fact that he opened the doors of freedom for millions of Americans.

EXERCISE 2: Rewrite the following composition, subtracting unnecessary words and ideas. Do not change the meaning of any of the sentences. Do not subtract important facts.

What About College

(A) ~~This composition will be about~~ college on account of the fact that hardly a day passes during which I do not hear the word *college* mentioned at least once--by a teacher, a friend, or my parents. In this day and age of such a technological world as today is, it is said that one can get nowhere in the business world if he does not have that all important piece of paper, also called a college diploma. Without the piece of paper called a diploma, you are nothing. With the diploma, you are common--like all other young people entering the technological world of today. What I mean to say is that everybody's got a diploma.

(B) But exactly what is college? Well, twenty or more years ago in the late sixties, college was considered a place for nothing but sports on account of the fact that "Joe Smoe" was the captain of the football team and was worshipped as a god. The intellectual and bright student who attended college to receive an education was laughed at, ridiculed, scorned, and made fun of. He was nothing but a bookworm, a person who always had his head in the book. In this day and age almost the reverse is true. The true student is looked upon with great respect, whereas the jock has definitely taken a back seat.

(C) In my opinion I think that college is definitely more than a higher high school. It is a place where the final change from childhood to adulthood takes place, changing boys and girls into men and women. It is a time when we make the deepest imprints on our character, the character with which we will have to go through life, the character that will show exactly what types of people we are. Sure, this change in a person does not have to take place without someone going to college, but college moves it along much more rapidly and swiftly. Needless to say, then, I think that college is the most important phase of our early lives, a phase that should be regarded with complete soberness and levelheadedness.

IDENTIFYING AND CORRECTING RUN-ONS

A run-on sentence is two or more sentences written as though they were one sentence. The writer simply "runs" two or more sentences together without proper punctuation.

Example: The Darien Rotary Club ran a raffle to raise funds for the needy in the community it was a great success.

Obviously, the end of the first sentence is after *community*, and the second sentence begins with *it.*

A good way to check for run-on sentences is to read your sentences aloud to hear the natural "pause." If you hear a pause, check for proper punctuation.

Example: Doctor Hamby cut off the bandage from Patrick's head he then cleaned the wound.

In reading the above sentence aloud, did you hear the pause between *head* and *he*? **Run-on**. No punctuation.

In analyzing column four on your **Sentence Opening Sheet**, see if some of your sentences are too long. Read them aloud or have someone read them aloud to you. This will help you "hear" not only the repetition of unnecessary words but also the "pause," a possible hint that you have a run-on sentence.

RULES FOR CORRECTING RUN-ONS
Here are five ways to correct run-on sentences:

1. Use a period (.) as an end punctuation. Capitalize the first word of the second sentence.

    Cooking a turkey on a Weber grill for Thanksgiving dinner takes several hours it has to be started early in the morning.

    Cooking a turkey on a Weber grill for Thanksgiving dinner takes several <u>hours</u>. **It** has to be started early in the morning.

2. Use a comma (,) plus a coordinating conjunction, such as *but, or, yet, so, for, and,* and *nor.* Just remember the expression **BOYS FAN**.

    I asked Melissa Cahill to the homecoming dance, she told me I was too fat.

    I asked Melissa Cahill to the homecoming <u>dance</u>, **but** she told me I was too fat.

Special Hint: A comma by itself does not connect two sentences.
A coordinating conjunction is needed. This error is called a comma splice.

Hundreds of Bulls' fans had been waiting in the frigid temperature for hours, they wanted to buy tickets to the championship game against the Suns.

Hundreds of Bulls' fans had been waiting in the frigid temperature for hours, **for** they wanted to buy tickets to the championship game against the Suns.

Hundreds of Bulls' fans had been waiting in the frigid temperature for hours. **They** wanted to buy tickets to the championship game against the Suns.

3. Use a semicolon (;) if the two sentences are closely related in meaning.

The Bunker family often argued in public no one seemed to care.

The Bunker family often argued in public; no one seemed to care.

4. Rewrite the sentence by subordinating with subordinating conjunctions, relative pronouns, or present participles. Punctuate correctly.

The family searched for mushrooms in the forest they found hundreds near the cave entrance.

As the family searched for mushrooms, they found hundreds near the cave entrance. **(Subordinating Conjunction)**

The family **that** searched for mushrooms found hundreds near the cave entrance. **(Relative Pronoun)**

The family searched for mushrooms, **finding** hundreds near the cave entrance. **(Present Participle)**

5. Use a conjunctive adverb such as *consequently, however, moreover, therefore,* and *nevertheless* to introduce the second sentence. A semicolon (;) comes **before** the adverb; a comma (,) follows.

Katie tries to practice her free throws every day, she doesn't always have time.

Katie tries to practice her free throws every day; **however,** she doesn't always have time.

EXERCISE 3: On a separate sheet of paper, correct each run-on sentence.

1. Students in Mrs. Suchor's English IV class work in small support groups for peer evaluation this gives them a chance to learn from each other.

2. Coach Washington continued to discuss the effects of the playoff loss until late in the evening, nobody told him that he missed the team bus back to school.

3. Representative Savage was absent when his education committee vote took place, he had enough votes so it passed by a comfortable margin.

4. The maestro's ring fell off of her finger, it dropped into the orchestra pit.

5. I left the check at the office, you can pick it up tomorrow morning.

6. Jessica was accepted at Harvard University she preferred to attend St. Mary's College instead.

7. The student council voted to postpone the student election the decision was not popular among the students.

8. Ishmael was strolling leisurely on the deck a huge wave washed him overboard.

9. President Clinton signed the bill, it caused happiness among the civil rights workers standing outside the White House.

10. I tried out for the debate team three straight years I never made it.

11. Maureen excitedly walked down the aisle her palms sweated as she clutched her bouquet.

12. I was a little nervous as I began my presentation I did not create a good impression.

13. We arrived in Twisp just in time for the chili cookout I left all my pots and pans back in Bellevue.

14. James Brook's new movie received terrible reviews, it was a huge success at the box office.

15. Wendy was smiling sweetly at her mother, she asked for permission to attend wrestling mania to see the "Hulkster."

16. The two teams lined up for the "Star Spangled Banner," then the game began.

17. I knew that Matthew Thomas would do a good job, in every position he has ever held he has always performed excellently.

18. Zig's assignments always look neater than anyone else's in the class, he uses his friend's LaserWriter printer.

19. Our family likes to preserve our Slovak traditions on Christmas Eve, this makes us feel closer.

20. We stayed at the Bremen Theater for the second movie, then it was too late to attend the Sandburg basketball game.

VARYING SENTENCE LENGTHS

Varying your sentence lengths increases the effectiveness of your writing. If your sentences are too short, they sound choppy. If your sentences are too long, they are monotonous and uninteresting. Variety is the key. An effective way to emphasize an idea is to include a short sentence among longer ones.

EXERCISE 4: Rewrite the following paragraph, using a variety of sentence lengths and openings. Subtract unnecessary words and ideas.

1 . I was strolling to my girlfriend's house one summer day. 2. I heard the rattle of a chain. 3. I turned around, and I found myself trailed by a vicious looking dog, a pit bull. 4. I tried to maneuver myself away from this dog, and all of a sudden I realized that I had a bigger problem than I had anticipated.

5 . I tried yelling for a neighbor, hoping that someone would hear me and come to my rescue, but no one heard me. 6. I was in a state of frenzy, and so I decided to walk as fast as I could without running, and I hoped that the pit bull would not follow me, but he moved wherever I went.

7 . I saw a dumpster in the distance near an abandoned building, and I decided to try to escape from the pit bull by climbing into the dumpster. 8. I was terrified, and I started to run, and the pit bull ran after me revealing his ferocious teeth. 9. I was screaming and running and finally made it to the dumpster. 10. I jumped as high as I could so that I could try to climb inside.

11. All of a sudden I heard a shrill whistle, and the pit bull stopped running after me. 12. I was inside the dumpster, and my heart was pounding furiously when I saw the pit bull run to his master, and I was never so relieved in my life.

REVISING OVERLY LONG SENTENCES TO EMPHASIZE MAIN IDEAS

Long, rambling sentences, containing too many ideas and usually connected by the coordinator *and*, make reading the sentences monotonous. Sentences like these produce dull writing. To achieve some quality in your writing, you must vary your sentence structures and sentence lengths.

You should not worry about variety in structures and lengths on your first draft. Just concentrate on ideas. However, as you become proficient in practicing the skills of **combining**, **rearranging**, **subtracting** and **expanding** ideas, your writing will improve. As your skills improve, you will have to spend less time revising.

EXERCISE 5:   Many of the following sentences ramble on. They are simply strung together with too many *ands*, *buts*, or *yets*. When you revise your sentences, coordinate and subordinate accordingly. You might have to divide some of the sentences into two or three shorter ones. Be prepared to explain your revised sentences.

Example: Paul Robeson High School is the first urban school to participate in the Outcomes Accreditation Evaluation (OAE) program, ***and*** it has developed a strong curriculum to meet the needs of its diverse student population, ***and*** Paul Robeson has a dedicated staff of professionals willing to accept the challenges of an inner city school.

Revised: **(A)** With a staff of dedicated professionals willing to accept the challenges of an inner city school, **Paul Robeson High School**, the first urban school to participate in the Outcomes Accreditation Evaluation, **has developed a strong curriculum to meet the needs of its diverse student population.**

In model **(A)** the idea that Paul Robeson High School has developed a strong curriculum to meet the needs of its diverse student population has been emphasized because it expresses a complete thought by itself. The other two ideas have been subordinated, making them less important.

(B) The first urban school to participate in the Outcomes Accreditation Evaluation program, **Paul Robeson High School has developed a curriculum to meet the needs of its diverse student population. Its dedicated staff accepts all the challenges of an inner city school.**

Two ideas have been emphasized in model **(B)**. They both express complete thoughts. In revising the original *and* sentence, the writer wanted to stress two ideas and vary the lengths of her sentences. Consequently, she divided the original sentence into two sentences. What are the two ideas she stressed?

(C) Paul Robeson is the first urban high school to participate in the Outcomes Accreditation Evaluation program. Staffed by dedicated professionals willing to accept the challenges of an inner city school, Paul Robeson has developed a curriculum to meet the needs of its diverse student population.

In model **(C)** two main thoughts have been emphasized. The writer divided the original sentence into two sentences. What are the two ideas she emphasized?

TRY THESE:

1 . Chicagoans are hard working and aggressive people, **and** they are a mixture of all ethnic groups and races, **and** they are fighting to keep the human dignity of all their people, **and** they love the Chicago Bears and the Chicago Cubs.

2 . Meaghan Wagner dreamed about the senior prom for over a year, and she planned on the exact dress she would be wearing, and she anxiously waited for "Prince Charming" to ask her to the prom.

3 . School cliques are tight-knit groups, and they have their own hierarchy of authority, and they have their own set of rules.

4 . A team of scientists associated with the National Medical Institute has discovered a new chemical component, and it protects animals against viruses, and the scientists are planning experiments, and they hope these experiments may lead to the prevention and treatment of viral infections in human beings.

5 . Most Americans are easily fooled by advertising, and they should examine every picture and read every word, and they would be less apt to be swept away by catchy phrases and fancy slogans.

6 . Cities of America are unique, and they hold seemingly contradictory distinctions, and they stand as monuments of progress, and they are symptoms of social disease, yet they are a living, breathing history of America's success, yet they reveal man's failure, misery, ignorance, and problems.

7 . Alfredo was lying on the beach, and he was strumming his guitar, and he was singing happily, and a two hundred and ninety pound bully kicked sand in his face.

To analyze: to examine the parts of a topic in order to understand the whole.

Probably the most common type of paper you will deal with in high school and in college is the **analysis paper**. In an **analysis paper** your purpose is to take a complex topic and break it down into its components. Practically any subject could lend itself to an analytical paper, from a literary topic to a political topic to a historical topic to a scientific topic.

For example, a literary analysis might explain the use of symbols in the novel *Lord of the Flies*. A political analysis might explain the specific reasons why President Roosevelt began the New Deal. An historical analysis might examine several key battles and their impact on the outcome of the Vietnam War. A scientific analysis from a chemistry class might explain the structure of an atom. Obviously, **analysis papers** are useful for many topics in many different courses.

STAGE ONE: PREWRITING

STUDENT LEARNING OBJECTIVES

1. The student will state the topic using a controlling idea (thesis).
2. The student will write an introductory paragraph that captures reader interest, introduces the subject, and indicates the paper's direction.
3. The student will organize the paper by dividing the topic into suitable developmental paragraphs (thought patterns).
4. The student will link paragraphs either by repeating a key idea or by using transitional words.
5. The student will maintain a consistent point of view throughout the paper.
6. The student will provide specific details to support the analysis.
7. The student will end the paper with a sense of finality by writing an appropriate concluding paragraph.

HELPFUL DRILLS

To analyze means to examine the parts of a topic in order to understand the whole. Two ways of analyzing are possible. One is to start with the whole and separate into the parts (deductive reasoning); the other is to start with the parts and advance to the whole (inductive reasoning). The following two exercises demonstrate each type of reasoning.

EXERCISE 1: (Deductive Reasoning) Select a specific television program and analyze why this program consistently ranks as one of the top shows according to the Nielsen Ratings. With your class or in a cooperative learning group, discuss the show's popularity.

1. Is the program popular because of a special character or characters? What qualities does the character or characters possess that make them likable or detestable?
2. Is the program popular because of the plots? Are the plots full of suspense? conflict? adventure? laughter?
3. Is the program popular because of the guest celebrities?
4. Is the program popular because of some special feature, such as its music, special effects, setting, or timeliness?
5. Is the program popular because of the advice it gives? Or because of the lessons to be learned? Or because of the entertainment it provides?

After you have discussed each of the parts of the show, put your ideas together to see what makes the program popular. Plan how you would organize a paper explaining the show's popularity.

EXERCISE 2: (Inductive Reasoning) Read senior Mary O'Malley's analysis paper of what makes a teenage boy a "1." Then discuss what specific examples Ms. O'Malley used to arrive at her conclusion. On what qualities did she compare teenage boys? What was her basis for ranking each of the boys? What other ideas would you have added to support Mary's analysis? Finally, discuss whether or not you agree with Mary.

"1"

One afternoon a friend and I were discussing some boys we knew and were rating them on a numerical basis. Oddly enough, some of the good looking ones scored lower than the ones who were not great looking. Obviously, it was something much deeper than looks that made a "10" a "10."

I started thinking about what it meant for a guy to be a "10," and the qualities he should possess to rank as a "10." As I thought deeper on the subject, mentally listing a "10's" characteristics, I began to think about what it takes to be a "1" because I have met many of these geeks at Centennial High School.

Contrary to what many teenage girls think, looking like Mel Gibson does not automatically make a "10." A "1" is tacky. A "1" lacks class or style. He cannot master the art of saying the right thing.

A sure sign of a "1" is the lines he uses. Usually his smooth talk is either his best friend's or something he heard on a late night cable episode of *Baretta*. On a chosen Saturday night, when I spend two hours getting ready for a date, a "1" will inevitably ask, "What's all that junk on your face?"

Swearing is another good way of spotting a "1." Possibly some girls might find a constant stream of obscenities attractive. However, girls like myself, do not appreciate simple statements being told with four letter words interjected after every other word.

Also, a "1" possesses an overabundant amount of confidence, an inflated ego, and a definite cockiness. A "1" is the type who will wait until 5:45 P.M. on a Friday night to call for a date for that night. When he is refused, he nurses his bruised ego by asking for a friend's number.

A "1" is concerned with no one but himself. If the attention is not focused upon him, he pouts.

A "1" is either selfish and uncaring, or melodramatic and infantile. If he does not get his way, he becomes angry. If he is not flirting with another girl, he has tantrums because I am talking with someone else.

Generally speaking, a "1" is someone who cannot relate to people on their level. Even if he does not look like Mel Gibson or Billy Dee Williams, any male who can display a little sensitivity, warmth, and humor rates a quick "10." But for those, handsome or not, who cannot be congenial, they will always come up a "1."

Special Hint: Please note Ms. O'Malley's introduction. Because it tells a story, it is an "anecdotal" introduction. You may find a time when you would like to use this kind of introduction for a paper of yours.

WRITING PROMPTS

Many choices exist as subjects for your analysis paper. We are providing two general topics that you might select. As with the **definition paper**, writing across the curriculum options are also possible.

ADVERTISING: Choose your favorite magazine ad or TV commercial to analyze. No two students should select the same ad or commercial since there are plenty to choose from. Your purpose is to analyze the magazine ad or television commercial, pointing out the strategy the ad agency used to market the product being advertised.

A. Who is the ad agency trying to influence to buy the product? In other words, who is the target audience?
   1. Children, teenagers, yuppies, middle class, certain age groups, the elderly.
   2. Special interests groups: health conscious people, sports fanatics.
B. What marketing strategies did the ad agency use to make the product attractive to the consumer?
   1. Colors selected, setting used, situation developed.
   2. Humor, sentiment, economy, luxury living.
C. Did the ad agency use famous people? What characteristics do these individuals possess that make them attractive?
   1. Movie stars, models, sports figures, e.g., Hillary Duff, Tom Cruise.
   2. Experts: Charlie Trotter, Carl Sagan, Colin Powell.
D. Is the TV commercial shown at a special time of day? Why?
   1. Early morning, afternoon, prime time, late night.
   2. Saturday morning, Monday night.
E. Does the ad or commercial appear in a particular magazine or TV program?
   1. *Good Housekeeping, GQ, Seventeen, Newsweek, National Enquirer.*
   2. Soap operas, football games, cartoons, *60 Minutes.*
F. Does the commercial use special music?
   1. Top 40, Rock and Roll, fifties tunes, Beatles, _____.
   2. Classical, instrumental.
G. What kind of approach or special theme does the ad or commercial use?
   1. Reasonableness, entertainment, problem solving.
   2. "Get Your Man" or "Get Your Woman" theme.
   3. "Everyone has one," "Be the first in your crowd."

DILEMMAS: As a second general topic for the **analysis paper**, we want you to *analyze*, not narrate a specific problem. We want you to dissect a problem so completely that you can explain the *whys* of your topic. Your examples must be concrete. The purpose is to **explain**, not **narrate**. Here are some dilemmas that you might have experienced:

A. Analyze the difficulties a teenager encounters by not giving into peer pressure and going along with the crowd. (Discuss specific situations.)

B. Analyze the difficulties of not being able to use the family car or of being able to use the family car.

C. Analyze the difficulties of selecting the right college.

D. Analyze the difficulties of being an "outsider" and trying to become part of the school "in" group.

E. Analyze the difficulties of being the youngest member of the family and trying to compete with or "be like" your older brothers and sisters.

F. Analyze the difficulties of trying to live up to your parents' expectations or what you think your parents' expectations are.

G. Analyze the difficulties of trying to keep up your grades while participating in extra-curricular activities and/or holding a job.

H. Analyze a specific problem (your choice) and the difficulties this situation causes.

Other Possible Topics of Interest

1. Analyze the key components/characteristics of what it takes to be a good parent, a good teacher, a good student leader, a good (your choice).

2. Analyze a specific (your choice) college/university as an excellent school to attend.

3. Analyze the reasons why a specific political candidate (your choice) won or lost an election.

4. Analyze why different fads or trends have taken place in your city or in America:
   a. Rock and roll music.
   b. Particular clothes or hair styles, e.g., jeans jackets; the layered look; Reeboks.
   c. "In" places to hang out or go, e.g., malls, street corners, hamburger joints, someone's house.
   d. The development of the "rainbow coalition" in politics.
   e. Brainstorm other fads or trends.

5. Analyze "What if" happenings:
   a. Adolph Hitler had invaded England.
   b. Richard Nixon had not resigned as President.

c . President John Kennedy and Dr. Martin Luther King had not been assassinated.

d . Your braces did not come off in time for the prom as you expected.

e . You failed physical education and were not eligible to participate in extra-curricular activities.

f . Brainstorm other "what if" possible situations. Think!

ALTERNATE TOPICS--WRITING ACROSS THE CURRICULUM

Literature

1 . Analyze some aspect of a literary work such as: theme of *Of Mice and Men;* characterization in *Hamlet*; setting in *Out of the Silent Planet;* tragic characteristics in *Othello* and *Macbeth.*

***See **Units 12** and **13** for analysis papers dealing with *The Glass Menagerie* and *The Adventures of Huckleberry Finn.*

History

1 . Analyze the specific strengths President (your choice) brought to the White House.

2 . Analyze how the American (judiciary or legislative branch of government) affects our lives daily. (Limit the area of government you select in this analysis).

3 . The British were defeated both at Saratoga and Yorktown during the Revolutionary War. Analyze the strategies used by both the British and American armies that brought about the British defeat.

4 . Place yourself in the position of a writer for a London newspaper who is well read on both the English and Colonial propaganda prior to the publication of the Declaration of Independence, and who travels to the colonies to investigate reports of revolutionary activity. The Declaration of Independence is proclaimed while you are investigating the revolution. With today's knowledge of the events, the propaganda, and the acts of Parliament, assess the reasons and ideals present in the Declaration of Independence.

5 . Analyze an aspect in history: Chief Joseph's effect on U. S. Indian policy; Winston Churchill's attitude toward England's allies; President Reagan's reasoning for the Star Wars program.

Science and Mathematics

1 . Analyze a concept in science: the process of making a genetic cross; the structure of an atom; the process of writing a chemistry equation.

2 . Analyze the various processes for solving quadratic equations.

3 . Analyze how Pythagorean mathematical and religious beliefs affected the development of mathematics.

BRAINSTORMING YOUR TOPIC

After selecting a topic, you must think through your choice to see if you know it well enough to analyze specifically and completely in order to write a well developed composition. This is an important step in the writing process. You will be totally frustrated if you choose and stick with a topic you are not capable of analyzing.

Rather than concentrating on a specific number of words, begin thinking of ways of developing your analysis. It is easier to think about a specific number of ideas rather than 500, 1,000, or 2,000 words.

From the outset you should concentrate on short term, manageable goals. Actually, you practiced this concept in your definition paper when you used a formal definition, examples, comparisons, negations, functions, synonyms, etc., as ways of defining your abstract word or phrase. Do the same thing with this paper. For example, the discussion suggestions on page 39 should help you determine your short term objectives for the analysis of a television commercial or newspaper/magazine ad.

THOUGHT PATTERNS

These short term, manageable goals are called thought patterns. Thought patterns are logical ways of dividing up a topic into developmental paragraphs. They are ways in which we think about things. They are logical paths the mind takes in categorizing and understanding ideas. Therefore, they can be useful to you in organizing the body of your analysis paper in two ways.

First, as you are brainstorming on your **Think Sheet**, thought patterns can prove helpful in organizing your analysis. In an analysis paper dealing with the adverse effects of violent television programs on viewers, you might include developmental paragraphs using the cause-effect thought pattern. For example, high school football players died by laying in the street after seeing the film *The Program*. A terrible incident in real life was caused by a violent movie portrayal. This is an example of a cause-effect thought pattern.

Second, different thought patterns can be used for the organization of individual developmental paragraphs. Dealing with the same topic, one paragraph might point out the "relationship" of specific television shows; the second might show how specific television programs "cause" undesirable behavior on the part of viewers. The third paragraph might illustrate "negative" characteristics upon viewers, and so on. Using **thought patterns** can be a valuable skill once you have learned how to apply them.

Here are some **thought patterns** that might prove helpful when you start to brainstorm on the topic for your **analysis paper**:

1. Cause-Effect

Cause-effect refers to a specific relationship between events. The first event caused the second event to occur.

Example: In writing a political science paper analyzing the reasons for Harold Washington's being elected the first black mayor of Chicago, you might analyze the causes that led to his election.

2. Functions or Roles

In the **definition paper**, you might have used functions as a method to define your abstract term. Functions or roles can also be used to develop ideas in an **analysis paper**.

Example: A literary analysis paper might show how the separate functions of plot, setting, and character combine to create the tone in Jack London's short story "To Build a Fire." An analysis paper outlining the qualities of a good coach might explain the functions of a good coach, i.e., as a teacher, as a parent figure, as a role model, etc.

3. Characteristics

Characteristics are another useful way of dividing up a topic. Characteristics are the traits, features, or qualities that identify a person, object, organization, etc.

Example: In a political science paper analyzing why a political candidate was or was not elected to a specific office, you might analyze his characteristics, dominant personality traits.

4. Conditions

Conditions are the qualifications, prerequisites, or situations that cause predictable results.

> *Example:*   If you were writing an analysis in which you were pointing out the conditions necessary for a successful school play, you would use conditions as ways of dividing up your topic.

Thought patterns are difficult concepts to understand. However, they are excellent guides to help you in organizing long compositions. In writing your **analysis paper**, consider the patterns listed here plus the ones from the **definition paper**, pages 2-7. Examples, illustrations, and negation might prove helpful in this assignment.

THINK SHEET

Now you need to brainstorm to see if you know enough to write a complete analysis.

Before you fill out the **Think Sheet**, sit down and talk your subject through with a classmate, your girlfriend or boyfriend, anybody who will listen. Talking it over will help you when you put your pen to paper.

You might want to record your conversation. Your teacher might even have you exchange **Think Sheets** before you begin writing your first draft.

If your teacher feels that the class is having difficulty in selecting topics, she might want to complete a group **Think Sheet** as a demonstration of what to do.

As you are completing your **Think Sheet**, make your examples concrete. Avoid generalities. Support your purpose with specific information.

Analysis Paper Think Sheet

1. Subject of the Analysis Paper_____

_____

2. Intended Audience_____

_____

3. Writer's Purpose_____

_____

_____

4. Short Term Goal #1 and specific reasons, facts, examples, illustrations, etc.

_____

_____

_____

5. Short Term Goal #2 and specific reasons, facts, examples, illustrations, etc.

_____

_____

_____

6. Short Term Goal #3 and specific reasons, facts, examples, illustrations, etc.

_____

_____

_____

7. Short Term Goal #4 and specific reasons, facts, examples, illustrations, etc.

_____

_____

_____

_____

8. Short Term Goal #5 and specific reasons, facts, examples, illustrations, etc.

_____

_____

_____

9. Tentative controlling idea (thesis statement)_____

_____

_____

_____

10. With your specific ideas listed in numbers 4 through 8, arrange them in the order you intend to organize your developmental paragraphs. You might need to review the **Thought Patterns** on pages 42-44.

STAGE TWO: WRITING THE FIRST DRAFT

With your **Think Sheet** in front of you, write your first draft. Do not worry about grammatical and mechanical errors at this time. You will correct those types of errors when you edit your draft. Use your **Think Sheet** to help you remember the main points you want to include in the body of your analysis.

CONTROLLING IDEA

Once you have made decisions about the topic and the audience, you are ready to write a tentative controlling idea or thesis statement. It needs to be clear and to the point, broad enough to allow you to include what you know about your subject yet narrow enough to keep you from including ideas that are not necessary. The controlling idea should be written in one sentence.

Your wording will probably be adjusted and maybe dramatically changed by the time you write your introduction. However, this statement will give you some direction as you are thinking through your topic. This controlling idea will eventually be incorporated in your introductory paragraph.

Here are some sample controlling ideas from different types of student analysis papers in various academic areas. What is the **purpose** of each controlling idea?

- "Winning isn't the only thing, it's everything" has become a credo adopted by many high school football coaches which forces them to try to win at all costs.

- Teenagers today feel pressures that their parents did not face twenty years ago.

- The poet John Ciardi has successfully blended the elements of form, content, and style to write a masterful poem entitled "On Flunking a Nice Boy Out of School."

- The development of the electron microscope broadened the horizons of research in medicine and biology.

- Photosynthesis is not only vital for plants but also for humans.

- The Monroe Doctrine became a cornerstone of United States foreign policy by the late nineteenth century.

DEVELOPMENTAL PARAGRAPHS

For this writing assignment, write your developmental paragraphs, the body, **first** before writing your introductory and concluding paragraphs.

In the developmental paragraphs you should take the major divisions (short term goals) which you have established on your **Think Sheet** and begin to expand with more specific details. Your **Think Sheet** should help determine the number of developmental paragraphs or short terms goals you will develop in the body of your analysis paper and your overall organization.

COHERENCE (GLUING TOGETHER IDEAS)

Each developmental paragraph must be glued with the preceding paragraph. Normally the order of the paper helps carry the reader from one paragraph to the next, especially in narrative and process papers. However, in analysis papers the linkage is less obvious. Consequently, it is important for you to show the relationship of your ideas by smooth transitions of thought. Transition words are an effective way to indicate the shift from one main idea to the next. Here are some transition words that could be used in an analysis paper:

Transition Words for Analysis:	also, another, as a result, at last, first, next, consequently, finally, second, for example, for instance, furthermore, in addition, thus, too, therefore, to sum up, etc.

Another way of gluing paragraphs is through the **repetition of a key word** or **idea** which smoothly connects the two paragraphs. Notice in the student-example how the writer connects the second paragraph by repeating the idea of "mockery."

(1)   In Cervantes' attempts to satirize knight-errantry, Don Quixote evolves from a comical figure to a tragic person ridiculed for his idealism. At first the actions of Don Quixote seem laughable and are simply ignored. But as his fame spreads, he becomes an object of jest and exploitation. People welcome him not because of his beliefs or ideals but to hold him in ridicule. The Duke and Duchess entertain Don Quixote not out of pity or respect, but for the great chance to have some rare sport.

(2) WHEN SUBJECTED TO THIS EXTREME MOCKERY, Quixote
is no longer comical or entertaining but tragic. He is not allowed to believe in
his conviction without being tormented. Their constant ridicule forces him to
become a broken man who believes his life was wasted on insane exploits.

Each developmental paragraph should include the following:

1 . A **topic sentence** that supports the overall purpose of your analysis.
This topic sentence can be the first sentence, the last or clincher
sentence, or implied in the paragraph's development.
2 . A **definite organization** organized chronologically, logically, in an
order of importance sequence, etc. Thought patterns.
3 . **Transition words** should be used to link ideas. Besides transition
words, repeated key pronouns or key words can also be used.
4 . **Specific details** must be included that support the paper's overall
purpose. No assumptions. Quotations from experts or reliable sources
can be used to support your controlling idea.

Now write your first draft.

INTRODUCTORY PARAGRAPHS

Different types of introductory paragraphs are presented here,
including samples from literary analysis papers: direct statement of fact, definition,
examples or illustration, background information, exploration of commonly known
ideas, and quotation.

Select any type of introductory paragraph that suits your purpose, with
teacher approval, of course.

Direct Statement of Fact Introductory Paragraph

A direct statement of fact is an excellent way to introduce a subject of
a paper and capture reader interest. In concrete terms the writer simply states
exactly what will be proven in his analysis. Here is a student model from a paper
dealing with William Shakespeare's tragedy, *Julius Caesar:*

In his play *The Tragedy of Julius Caesar,* William Shakespeare presented the tragedy of three men and revealed how their tragic flaws in character caused their own demise. Julius Caesar was murdered by his friends and colleagues because his pride and vanity caused him to appear ambitious. Jealous and envious, Cassius committed suicide because he could not attain the power he sought after. Finally, Brutus took his own life because he realized he had acted against his own beliefs of honor and justice.

Definition Introductory Paragraph

In an **analysis paper** a definition of the subject is an effective way of introducing the paper. This enables the reader to have a simple grasp of the subject. This type of introduction also lends itself to organizing the paper since the terms of the definition may be taken one at a time and explained in the body of the paper. Here is an example of a definition of an organization:

Athletes for Better Education (AFBE) is a non-profit organization for the development of inner-city student athletes. To improve athletic skills, to increase academic proficiencies in reading and writing, and to foster a positive mental attitude are the goals of AFBE. These goals are accomplished through an intensive two week summer camp program.

Here is another definition introductory paragraph from a literary analysis paper dealing with the elements of the short story, "The Most Dangerous Game," producing a single effect:

A short story, which is a brief fictional narrative written in prose, is composed of four basic elements: plot, setting, character, and theme. The author of a good short story skillfully blends these elements to produce a lasting single effect on the reader. Richard Connell accomplished this in his short story, "The Most Dangerous Game." By blending plot, setting, and character, Richard Connell has managed to leave the reader with a feeling of mystery by requiring the involvement of the reader's imagination in many parts of the story.

Example or Illustration Introductory Paragraph

The use of an example or illustration to explain a generality which will be proven in the body of the paper is also an excellent way to introduce an **analysis paper**. Here is a student example from a literary analysis paper dealing with Ken Kesey's *One Flew Over the Cuckoo's Nest:*

Throughout history there have been ongoing wars between the oppressive forces of the establishment and the forces of freedom and individuality. On one side the establishment demands conformity to all principles it sets down while the individualists allow, right or wrong, the freedom to make choices for this ongoing confrontation. An explicit portrayal of this battle is found in *One Flew Over the Cuckoo's Nest* by Ken Kesey. The battlefield was a state mental hospital, and the major combatants were Big Nurse Ratched, representing the establishment, and R .P. McMurphy, portraying the free spirit.

Background Information Introductory Paragraph

A background information introductory paragraph enables a writer to point out significant facts that the reader should know before the controlling idea is introduced. Here is a student model:

Alexander Solzhenitsyn was born in 1918. He studied at the University of Rostov and served in the Russian Army during World War II. In 1945 he was arrested and put in a labor camp for eight years because he was accused of making a derogatory statement about Joseph Stalin. He was released in 1953 after Stalin died. In his spare time he started to write. His first published novel recounts his experiences while he was imprisoned in the labor camp. Alexander Solzhenitsyn creates a mood of anger in his novel *One Day in the Life of Ivan Denisovich.* This mood of anger stands out through the frustrations of the prisoners, the brutality of the guards, and the severity of the camp rules.

Exploration of Commonly Known Ideas Introductory Paragraph

Another type of introductory paragraph that captures reader interest and informs him about the subject is an exploration of commonly known ideas. The writer simply reminds the reader of what he already knows. For example:

Advertising is a unique thing. Besides helping to sell different types of products, many ads have another side to them. If you turn on your TV for even a short glimpse of a commercial, chances are you just learned about a new word, an historical event, or have even seen a replica of a famous piece of art. These are just a few of the many different kinds of things that can be learned by watching commercials. It's really kind of funny, when you think about it, the advertiser is paying millions of dollars to get a little bit of education across with his product. In fact, it's like going to school with your TV.

51

Quotation Introductory Paragraph

A quotation can also be an effective opening to an **analysis paper**. You must make sure, however, that the quotation relates directly to the purpose of your paper and that it comes from a reliable source to reinforce your main idea. You must also indicate how the quotation ties in with your subject. Here is a student sample from a literary analysis paper on Joseph Heller's *Catch-22* :

> "They began to follow us around. They would try to guess where we were going to stop next and would begin drilling before we even got there, so we couldn't even stop. As soon as we'd begin to unroll our blankets, they would kick us off." These words spoken by Chief White Halfoat, a swarthy half-blooded Creek Indian from Oklahoma, demonstrated that the institution of big business possessed a ruthless spirit of expansion. In the superb novel *Catch-22*, the author, Joseph Heller unceasingly ridiculed and mocked the institution of big business in three ways--the "legendary" oil men of Chief White Halfoat, the vast business syndicate of Milo Minderbinder, and the exploits of Doc Daneeka.

CONCLUDING PARAGRAPHS

The purposes of concluding paragraphs are to indicate finality, to summarize a lengthy and complex analysis, to create impact upon the writer's stance, or to evaluate the material analyzed. The two types that are included in this unit are a quotation concluding paragraph and a summarization concluding paragraph. Both models are from literary analysis compositions.

Quotation Concluding Paragraph

If you end your paper with a quotation, you must make sure that the quote blends in with the paper's meaning. Too frequently students are frustrated in writing a concluding paragraph and just "tag on" a quote to end the paper without explaining its significance.

A quotation can be an effective ending if you use a reliable source to support your controlling idea. It would be foolish to quote from an unknown source or to use an ineffective quote since this is the last impression your reader remembers. Here is a student example of a good concluding paragraph from *The Scarlet Letter:*

Hester's sin of adultery was a sin of passion and was openly admitted which distinguishes her sin from Arthur Dimmesdale's and Roger Chillingworth's. Arthur committed the same sin of adultery as Hester, but he held it inside himself for seven years. Chillingworth's sin was merciless revenge. He unjustly punished Arthur until he died. His sin was summed up well when Dimmesdale told Hester, "We are not, Hester, the worst sinners in the world. There is one worse than even the polluted priest! That old man's revenge has been blacker than my sin. He has violated in cold blood the sanctity of a human heart."

Summarization Concluding Paragraph

Normally a summarization is used for extremely long papers. However, it can be used effectively to reinforce main ideas analyzed in the developmental paragraphs. Here is a student model from a literary analysis paper dealing with the theme of blind acceptance of tradition in Shirley Jackson's short story, "The Lottery":

The villagers blindly accepted the lottery not even thinking about the harm which it did to themselves. Also they never actually knew the reason why they performed this ritual year after year. In addition, the people did not even want to do so much as to disturb the tradition represented by the black box, let alone the entire lottery. As a matter of fact, they never even changed the date or time of the lottery. Even after someone close to one of the townspeople drew the black dot, condemning him or her to death, the people still did not attempt to bring an end to this inhumane ritual. The people only thought that there had always been a lottery, so why stop it now.

SENTENCE OPENING SHEET

After you have written your first draft including your introductory and concluding paragraphs, fill out the **Sentence Opening Sheet** as directed by your teacher. See an explanation from **Unit 1** pages 18-20.

PEER EVALUATION USING A CHECKLIST SHEET

Peer evaluation is an effective way to improve writing skills. You will be reading a fellow student's composition dealing with the same type of assignment that you wrote. Sometimes it is easier to spot mistakes on someone else's paper before you rewrite your own first draft.

In checking over your partner's assignment, focus on the stated objectives as listed on the **Student Objectives and Evaluation Sheet (SOES)** distributed by your teacher in the prewriting stage.

Since you have already studied an analysis paper dealing with the topic of what makes a teenage boy a "1" on pages 37-38, we have included a literary analysis model. Before you exchange papers with your proofreading partner, read and discuss the composition which follows. It deals with *Antigone,* a popular Greek drama. Use the guide questions from the **Checklist Sheet**, page 56.

Creon, tragic hero

(A)   In his play *Antigone,* Sophocles portrayed the Theban king Creon as an unreasonable, selfish, and tyrannical ruler. At first he appears as the villain, bent with the intention of destroying the heroine Antigone. His judgments seem rash and unjustified. Yet when we analyze his actions, the character Creon resembles the tragic hero described by Aristotle in his work *Poetics.*

(B)   For Aristotle, the tragic character has to affect many people beyond himself. Usually a king would be considered as the most effective. In this manner Creon had an effect on the people of Thebes. He now acted as king after the two previous heirs, Eteocles and Polyneices, had met and killed each other in a great battle for the throne. The Thebans looked to Creon for guidance and leadership.

(C)   Another quality Aristotle emphasized in a tragic hero is that his background should not be all good nor all bad. The idea is to have the audience identify themselves with the tragic hero. Whereas the downfall of a virtuous man would shock the audience and the downfall of an evil man would please them, the downfall of a man neither all good nor all bad would bring down the proper emotional response. Likewise, Creon acted neither as a virtuous man nor as an evil one. He demonstrated his lack of virtue in the earlier parts of the play with such actions as the disgracing of Polyneices' body and his treatment of the defiant Antigone and his son Haemon. In his hopeless attempt to correct the situation which he created, Creon displayed that he was not completely evil.

(D)   Aristotle also included a reversal of intention or fortune. In such a reversal "the action veers to its opposite." Creon's reversal came when he, once the oppressor, ended up the oppressed, persecuted by the deaths of Eurydice, his wife, and Haemon, his son.

(E)   According to Aristotle, the tragic character had to experience a recognition scene. During such a scene the truth becomes evident to the unaware hero. Creon experienced such a scene. With the advising of the blind prophet, Tiresias, Creon realized the horror of his deeds. Afterwards he moved to correct his error, only to find it too late.

(F)   The most important element evoked by a tragedy is the catharsis, or the emotional response of the audience to the tragic hero's plight. The proper tragedy should draw a catharsis of fear and pity. Without his catharsis the tragedy is a failure; the whole purpose of the tragedy is to obtain the catharsis. The catharsis for the play *Antigone* matches that which Aristotle required. The fear that is felt is for Creon's fatal mistakes, a fear that they may be committed by us. The origin of this fear is not only in the possibility of the mistake happening to any of us, but also in the painful consequences. The pity for Creon is felt in that in his attempts to do what he felt was right for the state, he violated a greater law and in the process destroyed his entire family.

(G)   Though he plays the role of the antagonist, Creon truly is the tragic character of *Antigone*. His character seen through his actions matches every aspect of the tragic hero set down in the *Poetics*. Sophocles summed up the tragedy of Creon in the last lines of his play:

> But high and mighty words and ways
> Are flogged to humbleness, till age,
> Beaten to its knees, at last is wise.

Writer's Name_____

Evaluator's Name_____

Analysis Paper Checklist

Introductory Paragraph

1   How does the writer's opening paragraph capture your interest?

2 . What is the subject being analyzed? What is the writer's purpose?

Developmental Paragraphs

3 . How has the body of the composition been organized to support the writer's purpose? What **thought patterns** has the writer used?

4 . If the writer included any ideas that digress from the topic, indicate this on the first draft.

5 . Mark the transition words or repeated key phrases, words, or ideas used to make a smooth transition between paragraphs.

Concluding Paragraph

6 . What type of concluding paragraph did the writer use?

Style and Form

7 . Which sentence openings need to be rearranged to add interest to the composition?

8 . Which sentence lengths need to be varied to emphasize key ideas?

9. What point of view did the writer use in his composition? Is he consistent? If not, mark the shift in point of view on the first draft.

Mechanics

10. Reread your partner's paper checking for the following errors: fragments, run-ons, verb tense consistency, spelling, punctuation, etc. **Be a friend!**

FINAL COPY AFTER PEER EVALUATION

Before submitting your final "neat" and error-free copy, follow the same procedure you used in revising your **definition paper**. Make sure you reread your final draft aloud three or four times, each time concentrating on one specific objective: spelling, punctuation, specific details, etc.

As a final check, evaluate your final draft based on the student learning objectives as stated on page 36 of this unit and the **SOS** sheet. If you discover something that needs to be corrected, do it.

STAGE FOUR: PUBLISHING

One publishing activity for this assignment might be to present your paper to another class, especially if you have selected a writing across the curriculum topic.

An oral presentation or speech is another publishing possibility.

Finally, you might select this paper for your writing portfolio.

A verb is a word that expresses action or state of being. It is the word that breathes life into a sentence. It reveals movement, thoughts, inner feelings. Without verbs, there would be no sentences.

The purpose of the third column on the **Sentence Opening Sheet** is to make you aware of the verbs that you have written on your first draft. Being aware of your verb selections will aid you in revising your sentences to make them more meaningful.

First Four Words Per Sentence	Special	VERB	Number of Words Per Sentence
		is written	
		got	
		twisted	
		was	
		is	
		are	

VERB TENSE CONSISTENCY

When you have written your first draft, we have emphasized writing your ideas down as fast as you could without worrying about mechanical and grammatical errors. In following those directions, some of you might have shifted from present tense to past tense. That is okay. Your main purpose at that stage of the writing process was to get your ideas on paper without unnecessary interruptions.

In revising your first draft, however, you must make sure that your verb tenses are consistent. Otherwise, this shift in tenses will confuse your reader.

                              past   **present**

Example: Dean Mohan *saw* the problem months ago and *decides* to act upon it.

                              past   **past**

Revised: Dean Mohan *saw* the problem months ago and *decided* to act upon it.

EXERCISE 1: Read the composition aloud, and then change the tenses whenever necessary to keep them consistent. All the verbs should be written in the past tense.

The Battle

1. The three little "monsters" whom I baby-sat for last Saturday evening drive me crazy. **2.** When I first mention "sleep" at 8:30 P.M., they moan and groan at me. **3.** Since their folks were not returning home until after midnight, I realize one huge mess awaited me.

4. First, I tried to be nice by talking to them calmly and suggesting that they go to bed after watching a cartoon video their folks had rented for the evening. **5.** This does not work. **6.** They said that they were going to stay up as long as they wanted, and they began screaming their lungs out, demanding more pop and chips.

7. I decide to threaten them, telling the little creeps that I was going to call their parents at the number they had left me. **8.** It was a bluff, and the kids know it. **9.** If I told their folks how ornery they were acting, they said they were going to tell them that I had brought my boyfriend over to help with my homework. **10.** The kids knew I was not allowed to have anyone visit me, and they are going to take advantage of the situation. **11.** I feel totally frustrated.

12. Since they were going to lie to their parents about me anyway, I decide to just pick them up and drag them to their rooms. **13.** I was not going to let them beat me. **14.** So I did it. **15.** Their screaming and crying drive me nuts, however, so I bring them back out to the living room and decide to let them watch TV. **16.** I feel beaten.

17. Finally, I came up with the ultimate plan. **18.** Why not play games with them, running around the house with them until they get exhausted? **19.** So, I tried it. **20.** It works. **21.** They become so tired from our games of "Wolf-Wolf" and "Hide-and-Seek" that they fall asleep on the couches in the living room. **22.** I pick them up and carried them to bed. **23.** The battle is over. **24.** I won.

ACTIVE VOICE AND PASSIVE VOICE IN SENTENCES

When the subject of a sentence performs the action expressed, the verb is in the active voice. When the subject receives the action of the verb, the verb is in the passive voice. Since the *subject-verb-object* sentence pattern is the type most frequently used in English, active voice sentences are more common than passive voice ones. Here are some examples:

Active Voice: Chris **vacuumed** the basement rug after the flood.

Passive Voice: The basement rug **was vacuumed** by Chris after the flood.

Active Voice: Roger Reed **panned** the new Lucas-Spielberg film.

Passive Voice: The new Lucas-Spielberg film **was panned** by Roger Reed.

The passive voice is formed by using the past participle and some form of the verb *be: is, are, was, were, been,* etc.

- The new Bears' stadium **will *be* constructed** at 47th and Damen.
- The bill ***was* passed** by the senate without much opposition.
- Why my giving a Christmas homework assignment ***was* complained** about by my students is still a mystery to me.

The choice of whether you use active or passive voice depends upon your purpose in the sentence. As a rule, however, active voice provides more force, is more direct, requires less words, relies less on forms of *to be,* and sometimes is easier to understand. For example, here is the active voice version of the Christmas homework assignment sentence above:

- My students' complaining about my giving a Christmas homework assignment still **mystifies** me.

Mystifies is the active voice verb in the sentence. Notice that there are fewer words. The *was* has been eliminated, and the sentence makes more sense. Here are more examples:

Example: A good writer **spends** many hours revising a composition.
   (Active)

This sentence is much more forceful and direct than:

Revised: Many hours **will *be* spent** by a good writer revising a composition.
   (Passive)

60

In the preceding active voice example, the subject is active and performs the action. Just listening to both of these sentences should tell you that the active voice sentence is more forceful.

You still have the option of using passive voice, of course. And it should be used under the following conditions:

1 . The object or receiver of the action is more important than the doer.

Our school band **has *been* invited** to march in the Rose Bowl Parade.

2 . The writer wishes to emphasize the receiver of the action more than the doer.

The editors of the ***Interlake Gazette* *were* asked** to resign by the superintendent because of their recent editorial against censorship.

3 . The doer is not known.

Not much money ***was* stolen** from the bank.

As a **general rule**, use active voice more than passive voice.

EXERCISE 2: Rewrite the following sentences, changing active voice to passive voice, or passive voice to active voice. Add any necessary words.

1 . Many requests for personal appearances are turned down by Michael Jordan.
2 . A mysterious stranger changed Mr. Fanning's seating chart without his permission.
3 . With Coach Hughes' help, the football dummies were carried back to the gym by all of us.
4 . During my last semester at Enunclaw High School, a composition was written by me, and it was rated the best paper in the class by Mrs. Franchini.
5 . The reason that Herman left school was that he lacked money.
6 . "Let There Be Peace on Earth" was sung by the entire congregation at the conclusion of the service.
7 . Many agonizing nights are spent by seniors trying to decide on the right college to attend.
8 . Frank Thomas hit the ball over the roof of White Sox Park.
9 . Isiah has bought a new magazine about college basketball.
1 0 . They lowered the flag on City Hall to half-mast to honor Mayor Washington.

EXERCISE 3: Change the verbs from passive voice to active voice in the following composition. The first two passive verbs have been highlighted.

As a high school freshman, I **was invited** by Chad Studrock, a senior and captain of the football team, to the spring formal. I **was thrilled** by his invitation. My relationship with my friends was changed by this situation, however. The reason that I was feeling superior and stopped hanging around with them was that they were lacking "the cool" of upperclassmen. They were nobody, and I was somebody, and they were lined up against me. Two days before the dance, I was dumped by Chad. I was told by him that another girl was asked by him to the dance before I was asked by him. I was devastated by Chad. Fortunately, I was welcomed back by my good friends with open arms.

REPLACING WEAK VERBS

Strong, vivid, and specific verbs enliven your sentences. They dramatize the actions of your essay, making your reader see and understand what is important to you. Sometimes in your haste to write your first draft, you fail to use strong verbs and instead write the first verb that comes to mind normally forms of *be*, *do*, *have*, and *get*.

- Our summer holiday **is** over, and it **was** a miserable ending because of the weather.
- Vernell **did** a good job on the composition.
- Miguel **has** a friendly smile, and I saw him when I **got** into the room.
- I **got** a new software program for my birthday.

These verbs are necessary and vital to the English language. However, they often become *crutches* for inexperienced writers. Instead of the writer's trying to use an exact verb that demands thinking, he will rely on "ole faithful," taking the easy way out. Nonsense! Look at these:

- Our summer holiday **ended** on a sour note as the rains **wiped** out the last weekend.
- Vernell **aced** his composition.
- Miguel's friendly smile **greeted** me as I **walked** into the room.
- I **received** a new software program for my birthday.

Notice how much more visual the sentences are?

The third column of the **Sentence Opening Sheet** will help you spot these weak verbs. If you notice that you are using them too frequently, you will need to substitute more specific verbs when you revise your first draft.

Here are some general rules to follow:

(A) Substitute an action word for forms of **to be: is, are, was, were, been**.
*Rodriguez **was** sad* can be written *Rodriguez **hung** his head low after the loss.*

(B) Substitute a specific action verb in the sentence for forms of the verb **to do: do, did, does, done**.
*Aggie **does** her cooking on the hibachi* can be rewritten *Aggie **cooks** her meals on the hibachi* or *Aggie **hibachies** her meals.*

(C) Substitute any action word for forms of the verb **to have: have, has, had**.
*Regina **has** an enthusiastic manner when she teaches* can be rewritten *Regina **excites** her students with her enthusiasm .*

(D) Substitute a more specific verb for forms of **to get: get, got, gotten**.
*Ophelia **got** a new dress for the prom* can be rewritten *Ophelia **bought** a $500 Zigmon original for the prom.*

EXERCISE 4: Rewrite the following sentences, substituting specific verbs for forms of *be, do, have,* and *get*. Expand each sentence to make it more interesting.

Example: Rehana Ahmed **is** a good student.
Revised: Despite holding a part time job, Rehana Ahmed **excels** in all her subjects at Carl Sandburg High School.

1. Mrs. Wineblad **had** her 75th birthday without anyone knowing about it.
2. Alfred **did** a nice repair job on the boat house.
3. Cassie **does** the dishes every night.
4. Stacey **had** a good time in Europe this past winter vacation.
5. Jake **is** a hard worker.
6. Kim Soo **got** to brooding about his bad luck.
7. Little Ben Palermo **is** a devil.
8. On his way home from school, Franklin **got** run over by a semi.
9. The lobster **had** a funny odor.
10. Dianne **did** a nice job in organizing the workshop.
11. Cousin Tommy **is** the resident story teller on fishermen's weekend.
12. Barb and I **had** a late night dinner at Devono's.
13. Sean **was** late for the opening kickoff and missed the 105 yard kickoff return.
14. Sylvester **got** up at 11:30 A.M. just in time to watch "All My Children."
15. Brian and Danny **got** a light lunch of 28 White Castle sliders, six large orders of fries, and four chocolate malts.

Every day people are explaining and instructing, from the math teacher who explains a quadratic equation, to a sprinkler fitter who teaches an apprentice how to hookup a sprinkler system, to an accountant who helps a client fill out a 1040 form, to a mother who instructs her daughter how to make chicken paprikas, to a student who tells a friend how to conduct a lab experiment in chemistry. However, telling someone how to do something is not enough. You must also be able to write a clear and logical explanation.

Process papers can be divided into two major types. In the first type of process paper, your purpose is to explain **how to do something**: how to solve a word problem in an advanced algebra exam, how to use a word processing program in a computer science class, how to build a cabinet in a shop class, or how to set up a future retirement program in an accounting class.

The second type of process paper explains **how something is done** or **how something works**: how an alarm clock works, how a new law comes into existence, how the Toronto Blue Jays management built an organization envied by other baseball owners, or how paying a mortgage saves the homeowner more money than renting an apartment.

Writing a process paper is a great way of learning more about a topic. This should be easy for you since we are always informing interested listeners how to do something, what something is used for, or how something works.

STAGE ONE: PREWRITING

STUDENT LEARNING OBJECTIVES

1. The student will write a process paper by explaining how to do something or how something works.
2. The student will write an introductory paragraph that captures reader interest and clearly states the paper's purpose in the controlling idea.
3. The student will organize the paper in a step-by-step sequence.
4. The student will provide specific details so that the audience understands the steps in the process.
5. The student will end the composition with an appropriate concluding paragraph.

STUDENT MODEL

Writing about something you know well is one of the keys in this assignment. Before you select your own topic, read and discuss the student models which follow. Use the guide questions for your discussion.

Introductory Paragraph
1. What type of introductory paragraph did the writer use?
2. How did the introductory paragraph capture your interest?
3. What was the writer's purpose as stated in the controlling idea?

Developmental Paragraphs
1. How did the writer organize his ideas? Are any steps out of order?
2. What steps would you have added?
3. Which, if any, ideas seemed confusing?
4. Other than transitional words, how did the writer make a smooth transition between paragraphs?

Concluding Paragraph
1. What type of concluding paragraph did the writer use? How was it effective?
2. How did the writer summarize the main ideas?

Style and Structure
1. What sentence structures and lengths need to be varied to make the composition more interesting?
2. What point of view did the writer use in the composition?

Why Komechak?

(A)   The summer between my junior and senior year was the best three months of my life. Winning the high school summer league baseball championship. Hanging out at the park. Meeting Laura. We were in the same homeroom for three years, yet I hardly noticed her. I "bumped" into her that summer at the pool when I dove off the high board and nearly drowned her. We started to date. It was a great summer.

(B)   Anxious to find out what teachers I would have for my senior year, I walked into the school cafeteria in late August feeling like a senior who was going to "rule the school," a line I memorized after watching *Grease* ten times that summer. I almost dropped when I got my schedule. For one long semester at 8:15 A.M. I would be greeted by the "friendly" face of Mr. Komechak in College Composition. Why me? There were four other English teachers who taught that class. Why did I have to get stuck with Mr. Komechak?

(C)   As a freshman, I practically killed myself in his class. I worked harder than I have ever done before and since then. My reward? *B+*! Not an *A-*, but a *B+*. This time I was determined to *ace* his class.

(D)   I did. College Composition--*A+*. For all you seniors who face the challenge of Mr. Komechak in senior English, I have the magic formula for getting an *A* from the toughest grader at South High School.

(E)   The first thing I did was to scrounge the garage for the box which housed my folder from freshmen English. After finding it, I studied all my returned papers from his class to see if I repeated the same errors again and again. They jumped out at me like a sore thumb: "Vary your openings," "Avoid weak verbs which make your sentences dull," "Subtract unnecessary words. You are writing in circles, saying the same thing over and over again," "Write about personal experiences you have had." I knew that I needed to eliminate these same mistakes in senior English.

(F)   Every time Mr. Komechak introduced a major writing assignment, he emphasized selecting a subject we knew thoroughly or getting the topic from one of our other academic classes so that the assignment became a writing across the curriculum project. He stressed this point again and again. Consequently, every time I was able to select another subject area as a topic for one of my assignments in Mr. Komechak's class, I would peruse the textbooks from my other subjects to find possible topics for Mr. Komechak's class. I would also ask my teachers for suggestions. This worked perfectly. Not only was Komechak pleased, but I benefited from the other teachers' knowing I was writing about something from their classes. In fact, I learned more about those areas by writing a paper. My definition paper was the science term *environment* from Mr. Pusateri's biology class. My comparison/contrast paper dealt with the differences in the ways Ronald Reagan responded to the recession of the early '80's with those of Franklin D. Roosevelt's responses to the Great Depression of the early '30's.

(G)   I spent more time thinking through a topic than I had ever done before. As a freshman I wanted to write as fast as I could so that I would be finished. Sometimes I said the same thing in different words so that I could fill up space. Occasionally, this worked. Now I realized that I had to spend more time thinking through my assignments because they were getting more difficult and sophisticated. I would talk my assignment through with Laura, letting her ask questions as I was reading the paper aloud. This helped. If she did not understand something, she would ask me to explain it or give an example. My writing became more specific.

(H) Revising a first draft has always been a problem. Actually, I did not revise a composition in junior high school. My first draft and final draft were one and the same. Since I was a pretty good writer and a "nice kid," I could get away with that then, not in freshmen English with Mr. Komechak, however.

(I) I also relied heavily on the grading sheet Mr. Komechak distributed in the prewriting stage and the sentence opening sheet to revise my composition. Sitting in my bedroom, I would read my paper aloud two or three times to hear how it sounded. Did it flow naturally? Did I add unnecessary details? I checked each objective on the grading sheet to see if I accomplished it. If I felt I did just an "OK" job, I worked on my weaknesses.

(J) To be honest, I stopped completing the sentence opening sheet because I knew what to look for without having to fill it out. It was time consuming. I checked for sentence variety, tense consistency, verb power, and sentence length variety by just looking over the composition. Since Komechak was "big" on these errors, I made sure none of them appeared on the final draft. In fact, in most cases I subtracted all forms of *to be.* I tried to write every sentence in active voice. Why? He preached this!

(K) Often we would evaluate each other's first drafts in class in small support groups. Even if Mr. Komechak did not allow time for peer evaluation, I always had someone evaluate my composition. I was not afraid of criticism. We would sit around the cafeteria during lunch and exchange papers. The only problem with this location was that I would often have to rewrite my composition because of a ketchup or mustard stain. Komechak demanded perfect-looking final drafts.

(L) My final suggestion for getting an "A" from Komechak is scheduling a short conference with him as soon as you receive your first graded composition. The meeting serves two purposes. First, it enables you to understand his comments and to use them in writing your next paper. Second, and more important, Mr. Komechak knows that you are a student interested in improving your writing skills. When he sits down late at night trying to determine if you deserve a B+ or an A- on your composition, he might give you the benefit of the doubt. This is not "brown nosing." It is good thinking.

(M) After one hard semester with Mr. Komechak, I received my deserved "A" in College Composition. I felt proud of it. I felt prepared to handle any writing assignment any teacher would give me. My formula for success in Mr. Komechak's class was not magic. It was just hard work.

WRITING PROMPTS

You will write a process paper in which you either explain **how to do something** or **how something works**. It is possible to write a process paper which combines both of these if you are working with a machine. For example, in using an electric drill, you can tell what the operator does and how the drill works and accomplishes its task.

Select a topic from your own experiences or from one of your academic classes. Ask your teachers from your other classes to provide topics for this assignment. Maybe you can make this a writing across the curriculum assignment. Avoid writing a paper that can be explained in one simple paragraph like ones you may have written in junior high school, such as tying a shoelace or folding paper the Japanese way, *origami*. The following list may trigger your memory in deciding on your topic:

General Topics

1. How to complete a shop class project (your choice).
2. How to study for an exam in the "toughest" class you are taking.
3. How to take pictures with a CANON 35 mm.
4. How to train a dog to be house broken.
5. How to water ski on one ski in turbulent water.
6. How a championship organization should be built or was built, e.g., Pittsburgh Penguins, Chicago Bulls.
7. How to . . . (your choice): a special skill you have, e.g., playing an electric guitar, programming a computer, tuning up a car.
8. How to become a successful lawyer, doctor, pharmacist, etc. (You might need to do some research for this topic.)
9. How something is built (your choice) e.g., garage, patio deck.
10. How to get accepted at the college of your choice or how to get the most benefit from a college visitation.
11. How a specific organization operates, e.g., student government, National Honor Society, 4-H Club, etc.
12. How to use a specific tool (your choice) or explain how a specific appliance works (your choice).

English and Humanities

1. How to build a set for a play, e.g., *Death of a Salesman*.
2. How to analyze a poem.
3. How to write a personal character sketch on a college admissions form.

4. How to layout a newspaper page in a journalism class.
5. How to give a speech in front of the entire school.
6. How to use a movie projector properly without having the reel unwind on the floor.
7. How to make a vase in an art class--ceramics.
8. How to paint a self portrait.

Social Studies and Economics

1. How a specific presidential candidate (your choice) was elected President.
2. How the electoral college works.
3. How Congress passes a bill.
4. How the stock market works.
5. How to select the best stocks and bonds to invest in.
6. How the primaries and/or caucuses function to determine delegates for the presidential nomination of each party.

Science and Mathematics

1. How you solved a word problem in a mathematics class.
2. How to use a microscope in a science class.
3. How to set up a scientific experiment, e.g., biology, physics, or chemistry, using the scientific method.
4. How a (your choice) specific experiment works, e.g., biology, physics, or chemistry.
5. How a tornado or hurricane is formed.
6. How a specific part of the body works, e.g., knee, heart.
7. How solar energy can heat a home.
8. How phosphorous helps the body systems.
9. How transistors work.
10. How a small motor or machine (your choice) works.
11. How gases from a rocket propel a craft.
12. How a multi-stage rocket works.
13. How crude oil is obtained from shale through physical and chemical means.
14. How a baseball curves.
15. How binoculars work.

As a group, brainstorm other possible topics for this assignment.
If some of the suggested topics are too general, you might need to break them down
to more specific ones.

In choosing a topic for this assignment, think about several processes which
you have experienced. To help you select a topic, answer the following questions
for each choice:

1. What was my purpose in completing this process?
2. What materials did I use?
3. Who needs the same information? In other words, who needs
   to know how to complete this process? Maybe they could be
   my target audience.

PURPOSE AND AUDIENCE

As with the first two assignments, you must consider your audience in
writing a process paper. If your subject is highly technical, you might have to
define some terms, especially if you know that your audience is not familiar with
what you are writing about.

In his book *get an A out of college*, Clark McKowen suggests that the
writer think of his audience as being his eight-year-old brother or sister as he begins
to jot down ideas. Any time the writer feels his younger brother or sister will
question him about something, he simply adds more specific details.
This is a good tip to remember as you begin to complete your **Think Sheet**.

THINK SHEET

Before you begin to fill out your **Think Sheet**, discuss your topic
with a classmate. This will help you clarify some of the ideas before you
begin to write.

On your **Think Sheet**, jot down every idea you feel should be included
in your process. This gives you a record of data to analyze to see if you have
sufficient information to write a multi-paragraph assignment.

Process Paper Think Sheet

A. Identify the **subject**--how to do something or how something is done.

_____

_____

B. Name your **audience**.

_____

C. State your **purpose**._____

_____

D. List all the **necessary materials** to complete this process, i.e., tools, ingredients, etc.

_____

_____

_____

_____

_____

E. List all the necessary and logical steps.

1.

2.

3.

4.

5.

6.

7.

8.

9.

10.

11.

12.

13.

14.

15.

F. Tentative Controlling Idea (Thesis Statement).

_____

_____

_____

_____

If you find that you have a difficult time listing a sufficient number of steps to develop your topic adequately, discard the **Think Sheet** and begin again. To stick with a topic that you do not know will lead to a frustrating experience. This is especially true if you are selecting a topic from personal experience.

However, if the topic comes from a list of suggested topics in a writing across the curriculum assignment, your teacher expects more research. You will need to spend time in the library.

If you are satisfied with your **Think Sheet's** information, you are ready to organize your ideas into paragraphs. Even if all the ideas are arranged in a step-by-step sequence, you must divide the ideas into major divisions--paragraphs.

STAGE TWO: WRITING THE FIRST DRAFT

With your **Think Sheet** in front of you, begin writing your first draft. Do not be concerned with grammar and usage errors at this point. Just write. Let your ideas flow from your **Think Sheet**.

Write your developmental paragraphs before you write your introductory and concluding paragraphs, just as you did with the **Definition** and **Analysis Papers**. Why? It is much easier to write an introduction and a conclusion once you know the content of your paper.

Each developmental paragraph should emphasize one step in the process. For example, if you are writing a **how to do something** paper, one of the developmental paragraphs might deal with the materials needed. If you are writing a **how something works** paper about a specific organization, one of your developmental paragraphs might describe the object itself or might explain the group's purpose.

ORGANIZING THE PAPER

How to Do Something

Your ideas must be organized logically and as clearly as possible so that your audience can follow your explanation on their own. For example, if you wrote a paper about tuning up a car engine, your audience should be able to follow your directions in order to tune up their own cars. If you wrote a paper explaining how to set up a cheerleading pyramid, your audience should be able to go to the gym and build their own pyramid, hopefully without breaking their necks.

Since this is a multi-paragraph assignment, you should subdivide the steps into developmental paragraphs. Each step should be fully explained with specific details. Your ideas need to be organized in a step-by-step sequence without any gaps.

How Something Works

If the topic that you select deals with explaining **how something works**, for example, how your church or synagogue successfully provides leadership and support services for all its members, you would need to organize the body of your composition into specific, short term goals--**thought patterns**. You will need to consider what information your audience must know in order to understand your organization.

Here are some ideas:

- One paragraph providing a brief history of how the structure came about.
- One paragraph outlining the church's or synagogue's structure, pointing out how the structure is organized into committees.
- One paragraph explaining the purpose(s) of each committee.
- One paragraph explaining how the goals are accomplished.
- One paragraph explaining its effect(s) on the members.

It is much easier to think of specific goals that you want to accomplish instead of thinking of a specific number of words. Every time you are given a major writing assignment, always think of ways of dividing up your topic into short term, manageable goals, which make up the body of your paper.

COHERENCE (GLUING TOGETHER IDEAS)

An essential quality of a well-written composition is coherence, that is, the relationship of the ideas, one thought leading to the next. Since your reader cannot read your thoughts, you must lead him from one thought to the next. This is difficult because we often ramble our ideas, which seem organized to us. Unfortunately, the relationships are often entirely personal, but are **not** clear to the reader.

Each developmental paragraph must have its own coherence. There must also be a smooth transition from paragraph to paragraph. This coherence can be accomplished in two ways: first, the logical order of the step-by-step process; second, the skillful use of transition words. Here is a helpful list of transition words:

Transition Words : first, second, third, finally, thus, furthermore, moreover, next, in addition, again, then, now, while, gradually, etc.

POINT OF VIEW

In junior high school when you wrote process papers, your teacher probably suggested that you write in the second person point of view, using the pronoun *you*. This was to avoid your constantly shifting reference from first person ("I") to second person ("you") to third person ("he," "she," or "it"). This was your teacher's way of functionally teaching you how to remain consistent in your point of view.

In teaching second person point of view, your teacher also taught you how to use the imperative or command form of the verb. Therefore, your process paper sentences probably looked like this:

> **Brown** the ground chuck in a tablespoon of
> peanut oil until the meat is crumbly, but not hard.
> **Combine** and **add** the remaining ingredients.
> **Cover** and **simmer** gently for 30 minutes. **Serve**
> on a toasted bun. ("You" understood.)

Since one objective of that assignment was to teach second person point of view and the command form of the verb, the instructions were correct. However, for this assignment, you can shift your point of view from first person to second person to third person as long as you know what you are doing. Why? Your paper should not sound like a recipe.

Now write your developmental paragraphs.

INTRODUCTORY PARAGRAPHS

For this assignment your introductory and concluding paragraphs will be written after you have written your developmental paragraphs.

Your introductory paragraph should capture your reader's interest and let her know the direction of your topic. In the **Definition** and **Analysis Papers**, six different types of introductory paragraphs were presented, pages 17, 49, 50, 51, and 52. Two more are presented here.

In deciding upon which type of introductory paragraph to use, think of the best way of getting your target audience interested in your topic. What are you going to mention in your introduction that will peak their interest and cause them to read on? Consider these questions:

1 . Why does your audience need the information that you will be providing?

2 . What information did you include in your developmental paragraphs that will help you decide which type of introduction is best for this assignment?

Background Information Introductory Paragraph

A background information introductory paragraph provides information that is commonly shared by everyone. It enables the writer to highlight general facts the reader should know before the specific topic is identified.

In the example that follows, note how the writer first provided some general information about hobbies as a source of enjoyment before he addresses himself to the specific hobby of leather craft and boot-making, the topic of the composition.

Hobbies are fun and recreational activities, providing many hours of enjoyment for the industrious novice. Although many hobbies require special skills acquired from reading books or attending special classes, other hobbies demand no previous experience. Leather craft, one such hobby, not only permits ease in learning but also professional looking results as well. A simple boot pattern can be completed without much trouble.

Direct Statement of Fact Introductory Paragraph

In a direct statement of fact introductory paragraph the writer directly states the subject of his paper. In the following student example, note how the writer states the topic in the first sentence. In the final sentence of the paragraph, he outlines the main ideas that he will be presenting in the body of the composition. His goal is to teach the consumer three logical steps in purchasing a new automobile.

Every year thousands of people purchase new automobiles without properly assessing their automotive needs and financial situation. They become hypnotized by the dazzling ads in magazines or the seductive commercials on television. If they follow these three steps, they will ensure buying a car that is not only practical but also affordable.

CONCLUDING PARAGRAPHS

Since the concluding paragraph is the last information your audience reads, you want to make sure you leave them with a good impression. If your composition ends on a sour note, your audience will have a sour taste in their mouths. Consequently, you need to spend time thinking about how you want to end your paper.

Since you know the content of the developmental paragraphs and have worked on your introduction, writing a concluding paragraph is not as difficult as it seems. Before selecting the appropriate type of concluding paragraph for this assignment, study the student models.

Two model concluding paragraphs were presented on pages 18, 52, and 53 of the **Definition** and **Analysis Papers**. Three more are included here.

A Proposition Restated as a Proven Conclusion Concluding Paragraph

In the model introductory paragraph dealing with hobbies, the student-writer proposed that boot-making can be both a recreational and profitable hobby. Having specifically proven his thesis in the developmental paragraphs, the writer now restates his controlling idea as a proven conclusion.

Although the results are professional looking, no previous skill was required. Leather craft and many other hobbies like it can fill otherwise wasted hours with entertaining and financially rewarding recreation.

Summarization Concluding Paragraph

A summarization concluding paragraph highlights the major points developed in the body of the composition. This conclusion reinforces the main ideas by condensing the main points. Here is the student concluding paragraph about the correct steps in purchasing a new automobile.

Only when a consumer sits down and seriously considers his automotive needs, assesses his financial situation, and spends time studying dealerships will he be able to buy a car that is both practical and affordable. If he fails to do this and instead listens to the enticers from Madison Avenue, he will pay the price.

Finality Concluding Paragraph

Since a **how to do something** process paper is organized in a step-by-step sequence, a finality concluding paragraph is an appropriate way to end the composition. The last paragraph is the final step in the chronological development. Here is an example from a student composition dealing with the proper steps in changing a flat tire on an automobile:

Finally, after the car has been lowered to the ground, remove the jack and pound the hubcap back onto the tire with your fist or a soft rubber mallet. Then take the jack, lug wrench, flat tire, and mallet, if you have used one, and return them to the trunk. Your job is now finished, and you can go on your merry way, hoping that you do not get another flat tire until you have had the tire in your trunk repaired.

Before writing your introductory paragraph and your concluding paragraph, you might want to discuss your choices with your partner or cooperative learning group.

Write your introductory and concluding paragraphs.

STAGE THREE: REWRITING

SENTENCE OPENING SHEET

With your first draft finished, including the introductory paragraph and the concluding paragraph, complete the **Sentence Opening Sheet** for one paragraph of your composition. After analyzing this selected paragraph based on the objectives for each column on the **SOS**, quickly analyze the remaining paragraphs for the same objectives.

See pages 18-20 for an explanation of the **SOS Sheet**.

PEER EVALUATION USING A CHECKLIST SHEET

Before you exchange papers with your proofreading partner using the **SOES** sheet or the **Checklist Sheet**, your teacher might have you exchange **Sentence Opening Sheets**. You can analyze your partner's paper for the various symbols listed above each column. For example, above the first four word column you might see the symbol **VAR**, which represents *variety in openings*. Above the verb column **VT** represents *verb tense consistency*.

Write your responses from the **Checklist Sheet** questions on the writer's first draft. During your peer evaluation time period, discuss your observations with your partner.

Writer's Name_____

Evaluator's Name_____

Process Paper Checklist

Introductory Paragraph

1. How does the introductory paragraph capture your interest and make you want to learn more about the topic?

Developmental Paragraphs

2. If the writer wrote a **how to do something** paper, how did he organize his ideas? Are there any gaps, that is, missing steps?

3. If the writer wrote a **how something works** paper, how did he organize his ideas? Mark the transitions that connect the paragraphs on the first draft.

4. Mark any paragraphs that needed to be expanded with the symbol **SPEC**, which indicates **specific** ideas.

Concluding Paragraph

5. Why was the concluding paragraph effective?

Style and Form

6. Use the suggestions from the **Sentence Opening Sheet** and check your partner's composition for the items listed, e.g., variety in sentence openings, special vocabulary words, verb choice, verb tense consistency, sentence lengths, etc.

Mechanics

7. Correct the spelling and punctuation errors on your partner's paper.

FINAL COPY AFTER PEER EVALUATION

After you have exchanged papers with your partner or in your support group, revise your first draft based on your partner's or group's suggestions and your own self-analysis. Remember, *the reader is a slothful animal.* No assumptions.

When your final draft is completed, read it three or four times and edit it for spelling, punctuation, capitalization, and usage errors. Your final draft should be neat and as error-free as possible.

If spelling is one of your major problems, you might want to read your composition backwards one word at a time. This will enable you to concentrate on each word to see if it is spelled correctly.

If you continue to write fragments, read your composition backwards, starting with the last sentence first, etc. This will help you identify fragments since you will be concentrating on one sentence at a time instead of reading your entire composition.

Also, read each sentence beginning with the words **I BELIEVE THAT**. If the sentence sounds confusing, it is probably a fragment.

Example: Because Marcia forgot to return the call.

           I BELIEVE THAT because Marcia forgot to return the call . . .

Fragment!

STAGE FOUR: PUBLISHING

Undoubtedly many outstanding essays have been written by your class. Why not publish a How To Do booklet?

How To Do papers are also excellent topics for speeches. Volunteers might give an oral presentation and demonstration.

Finally, some students might decide to include their essay in their writing portfolio as an example of this writing mode.

Seldom do first draft sentences express exactly what the writer has in mind. He can improve on the quality of them by revising, especially if he has mastered the sentence manipulatory skills of **combining** and **rearranging**.

PARALLEL STRUCTURES IN SENTENCES

Equal ideas demand equal grammatical structures. One of the tasks of a writer is to indicate to his audience when ideas are equal in importance in his mind. He accomplishes this by writing equal ideas in the same structure whether in a sentence or in a paragraph.

A good writer learns to indicate this equality of thought through the use of equality of structures. This is called parallelism. This very equality of structures lends conciseness, harmony, and balance to the expression of thoughts.

Coordinating conjunctions, also referred to as **equal idea glue words** in other **Stack the Deck, Inc.** publications, indicate structural equality. These words *glue* equal grammatical structures.

Relationship	Coordinator
Contrast	**B**ut
Option	**O**r
Contrast	**Y**et
Results	**S**o
Alternative	**F**or
Addition	**A**nd
Neither	**N**or

To remember these coordinators, just think of the expression **BOYS FAN**.

Any time these words are used to join structures, the ideas must be of an equal nature in the writer's mind; consequently, the structures must be the same. For example, if you wanted to stress that Jessica enjoys three specific sports, you could write the following sentence with coordinated or parallel (*//*) ideas:

Jessica enjoys **skiing**, **tobogganing**, and **bobsledding**.

In this example not only are the ideas equal but also the structures. This example was a simple one because equal ideas and structures were conveyed in one word. Equal or coordinated structures, however, can be much more complicated. Here is another example of parallel structures with verb phrases:

> The nurses **prepared** the patient for the operation, **placed** him on the cart, *and* **wheeled** him to the elevator.

In the above example, three equal structures, verb phrases, are separated by commas and the coordinator *and*.

When two or more words or ideas are equal in the writer's mind, they should be expressed in the same grammatical structure. Here are examples of different types of parallel structures:

A.   Compound or Parallel Nouns

Polaris High School <u>and</u> *O'Fallon High School* will dominate the Illinois state girls' volleyball championship this year.

B.   Compound or Parallel Verbs

Principal Lighthall *welcomed* the incoming freshman class, *encouraged* them to take advantage of the counseling program, <u>and</u> *invited* them to visit her office if difficulties arose.

C.   Compound or Parallel Adverbs

Cautiously <u>yet</u> *confidently* Christie inched her way off first base.

D.   Compound or Parallel Prepositional Phrases

The joy of working with retarded youngsters could be seen *in the faces of the volunteers* <u>and</u> *in the smiles of the children.*

E.   Compound or Parallel Gerunds and Present Participles (ING WORDS)

Not *planning* ahead, not *setting* definite goals, <u>and</u> not *matching* goals to personality <u>and</u> temperament are some of the common mistakes made by people ready for retirement. **(Gerunds)**

Little Elvis, *unwrapping his Christmas gifts* <u>and</u> *throwing the paper* on the floor, smiled with delight. **(Present Participles)**

F. Compound or Parallel Relative Clauses (WH Word Clauses)

The student *who thinks through his subject* <u>and</u> *who plans a strategy in outlining his ideas* will write good essay exam answers.

G. Compound Sentence Using Coordinators

We allowed the students to elect their own discipline committee, <u>but</u> *we suggested that they use sound judgment in selecting the members.*

H. Series of Sentences

Perhaps man has taken advantage of science. Perhaps technological advances have become an excuse for man to stop living a real, human existence. Perhaps man prefers to sit back quietly and allow society to shape the course of his life. If so, life means very little now, and soon will mean nothing at all.

PARALLELISM IN *The Gettysburg Address*

The Gettysburg Address is a masterful example of the effectiveness of the use of parallel structures. Both the meaning of the words and the very rhythm of the structures convey the equality of the ideas expressed by Abraham Lincoln.

EXERCISE 1: As a class activity, read Abraham Lincoln's famous speech. Then identify the parallel structures used in each sentence. Discuss the effect of the parallel structures on the reader/listener.

The Gettysburg Address

Fourscore and seven years ago our fathers brought forth on this continent a new nation, conceived in liberty and dedicated to the proposition that all men are created equal.

Now we are engaged in a great civil war, testing whether that nation or any nation so conceived and so dedicated can long endure. We are met on a great battlefield of that war. We have come to dedicate a portion of that field as a final resting place for those who here gave their lives that that nation might live. It is altogether fitting and proper that we should do this.

But, in a larger sense, we cannot dedicate--we cannot consecrate--we cannot hallow--this ground. The brave men, living and dead, who struggled here have consecrated it far above our power to add or detract. The world will little note nor long remember what we say here, but it can never forget what they did here. It is for us, the living, rather, to be dedicated here to the unfinished work which they who fought here have thus far so nobly advanced.

It is rather for us to be here dedicated to the great task remaining before us--that from these honored dead we take increased devotion to that cause for which they gave the last full measure of devotion; that we here highly resolve that these dead shall not have died in vain; that this nation, under God, shall have new birth of freedom, and that government of the people, by the people, for the people shall not perish from the earth.

COMBINING IDEAS WITH COORDINATING CONJUNCTIONS

EXERCISE 2: Combine the following sentences by using coordinating conjunctions. Punctuate properly by putting a comma before the conjunction if two sentences are connected; otherwise, run-ons will result.

Example: Dr. Budz followed the instructions in the Frugal Gourmet's new cookbook. The cheesecake turned out better than expected.

Sentence: Dr. Budz followed the instructions in the Frugal Gourmet's new cookbook, **and** the cheesecake turned out better than expected.

1. Ginger cut the lawn for her grandmother. She did not rake the clippings.
2. Jason will have to take the SAT on March 18th at Everett High School. Jason will have to take it at Mariner High School on March 24th.
3. I wanted to tell Mary Allen my problem. I thought she would laugh in my face.
4. High school students should learn how to use a computer. Learning how to use a computer will be useful in college and help them in the work force.
5. The umpire thumbed the runner out. She jumped high into the air.
6. I wanted to become active in the Girls' Athletic Association. I decided to run for the President of the Sigma Phi Sorority.
7. The father should change the baby's diaper. The baby will have a sore bottom.
8. You should not look at your neighbor's paper during the exam. You should not look inside your desk.
9. Paul and Pat bought tickets to Cooperstown. They wanted to see Carlton Fisk enshrined in the Hall of Fame.
10. Most students love to sleep late on weekends. Their parents get angry when they do.

84

COMBINING IDEAS USING CORRELATIVE CONJUNCTIONS

Another group of coordinators that connect equal ideas occur in pairs. These words also serve as equal signs and connect equal structures. These coordinators are called **correlative conjunctions**.

Either... or
Neither... nor
Whether...or
Both..and
Not only.. but (also)

EXERCISE 3: Combine the following sentences, using correlative conjunctions. Make sure that you place the correlative conjunction before the parallel ideas being expressed.

Example: The thieves took all the watches in the showcase. They took all the precious gems from the safe.

Sentence: The thieves took **not only** the watches in the showcase **but also** the precious gems from the safe.

1. Olga may spend Thanksgiving returning to her homeland. Olga may spend Thanksgiving celebrating with her relatives.
2. The television audience did not enjoy the concert. The live audience did not enjoy the concert.
3. Emma Wagner won a gold medal for figure skating at the World Games in Prague. Emma Wagner signed a multi-year contract with the Ice Spectacular.
4. The boys will take the math proficiency exam on Friday afternoon. The girls will take the math proficiency exam on Friday afternoon.
5. If Shawna drinks chocolate malts, she will put on weight. If she drinks diet soda, she will put on weight.
6. At most of the better colleges throughout the country, a student must apply by December 1st of his senior year. He will not be accepted.
7. A driver should not drive aggressively. A driver should not drive timidly.
8. A person who is organized will succeed in school. A person who is organized will become a success in life.
9. You will scoop up your dog's poop. You will get a pooper ticket.
10. The principal congratulated the seniors on their school pride demonstrated during the homecoming festivities. The superintendent also congratulated the seniors.

PARALLEL IDEAS WITH VERBS

Another way of writing parallel ideas is to write a series of compound or parallel verbs having the same subject. In doing this, you subtract the unnecessary words and reinforce the sentence's meaning by the conciseness of the structure and the rhythm of the sentence.

EXERCISE 4: Combine the following sentences into one by using compound or parallel verbs. Punctuate a series of verbs properly.

Example: Kathy took the cover off the typewriter. Kathy hit the "on" switch. Kathy inserted erasable bond paper into the machine. She typed a letter for Mr. Cahreb.

Sentence: Kathy **took** the cover off the typewriter, **hit** the "on" switch, **inserted** erasable bond paper, and **typed** Mr. Cahreb's letter.

1. The American Red Cross **has spread** the spirit of America to underprivileged countries throughout the world. The American Red Cross **has assisted** the needy in times of crisis. The American Red Cross **has provided** supplies for disaster-struck areas.

2. Essay exams **give** students an opportunity to share their knowledge with the teacher. Essay exams **force** students to think through the subject. Essay exams **make** students organize their thoughts in a logical sequence.

3. Intramural sports **help** students to develop new skills. They **provide** an opportunity to meet new friends. Intramural sports **enable** students to develop a competitive edge.

4. Ms. Brookes heard the uproar in Room 312. Ms. Brookes walked into the room. Ms. Brookes peered into the eyes of the noisy students.

5. The seniors climbed onto the bus bound for Boston. The seniors looked for empty seats. They placed their luggage on the overhead rack.

PARALLEL IDEAS WITH VERBALS AND RELATIVE CLAUSES

Another way of writing parallel structures is by using compound verbals, **ING phrases,** either as present participles or as a gerunds.

Example: Public television presents a variety of cultural programs. It provides an opportunity to receive college credit at home. Public television enables viewers to acquire new skills.

Sentence: **Presenting** a variety of cultural programs and **providing** an opportunity to receive college credit at home, public television enables viewers to acquire new skills.

Relative clauses can also be used to combine parallel structures. They are introduced by relative pronouns: **who, whom, whose, which,** and **that.** They are called WH words throughout our series.

Example: Ingmar Burman's new movie received excellent reviews. It starred Tim Conway and Elizabeth Taylor. It was a failure at the box office.

Sentence: Ingmar Burman's new movie **which** received excellent reviews and **which** starred Tim Conway and Elizabeth Taylor was a failure at the box office.

EXERCISE 5: Combine the following sentences by using verbals (ING phrases) and/or relative clauses (WH words).

1 . Rosa Gonzales sat down at her desk. Rosa opened her psychology book. She pulled out a yellow marker to underline the key passages. She turned on a bright light.
2 . The trumpets were blaring. The drums were booming. The Eagles' marching band paraded in front of the homecoming court.
3 . Kelly lacked confidence as a freshman. He stuttered whenever he spoke. Kelly was elected president of the student council as a senior.
4 . The policewomen was driving down La Grange Road. She was listening to the police report. She spotted the burning car in Sears' parking lot.
5 . The Equal Rights Amendment speaker concluded her speech. She hurriedly and confidently walked from the speaker's platform. She accepted the applause.
6 . Millie relaxed on the couch. She switched from channel to channel. She found the program she had been looking for.
7 . The violent winds caused snow to drift over the highways. They forced a trailer ban on the interstates. The violent winds were clocked at 89 miles per hour.
8 . Jonathan chaired the faculty council. Jonathan asked everyone to make sacrifices for the good of the school. Jonathan implemented his program.

CORRECTING SENTENCES WITH FAULTY PARALLELISM

Often when students are in a hurry to write parallel ideas on their first draft, they inadvertently connect these ideas in unequal structures. The sentences sound awkward. This is called faulty parallelism.

Example: *To pronounce words* and *recognizing their meaning*
are the first steps in reading for comprehension.

The coordinator *and* connects the infinitive (*to pronounce*) with an ING phrase or gerund phrase (*recognizing their meaning*). One of the structures must be rewritten to correct the faulty parallelism. (*//*)

Revised: *Pronouncing words* and *recognizing their meaning* are
the first steps in reading for comprehension. (Or, to pronounce
and to recognize.)

Here is another example:

Example: Juanita is *beautiful, talented,* and *has a nice personality.*

Can you think of a single word which means *has a nice personality*? Proper parallelism results if *has a nice personality* is rewritten as *personable.*

Revised: Juanita is *beautiful, talented,* and *personable.*

EXERCISE 6: Rewrite the following sentences, using parallel structures to express parallel ideas. First identify the coordinating conjunction or correlative conjunctions and then check the structures being connected. Complete the first three as a group activity.

Special Hint: In correcting faulty parallelism sentences with correlative conjunctions, make sure that you place the correlative conjunction before the parallel ideas being expressed.

Example: Eric **not only** enjoys watching World Federation Wrestling on TV
but also building with Lego toys.

Revised: Eric enjoys **not only** watching World Federation Wrestling on TV
but also building with Lego toys.

1. To visit each teacher in the classroom, advising the principal as to the hiring of new teachers, and to develop curriculum are some of the responsibilities of a department chairperson at Bay Port High School.

2. With dreams of a college education and wishing to become an aeronautical engineer, Kris Kosek saved all of her money from her summer job as a carpenter.

3. Students going away to college should check that they have enough clothes to last two weeks and finding out if their roommate will bring a stereo.

4. The unruly fans booed the umpire, shouting vulgarities, and threw cups and crumpled paper onto the court to show their dissatisfaction with the call.

5. The pace of our modern world prevents the development and growing of an individual's personality.

6. Ashley enjoys science fiction programs with exciting action and which portrays life as it will be in the 21st century.

7. My dad told me that his pension check would be coming within the week and to buy the AM-FM radio as soon as possible.

8. Governor Joan Kavanaugh changed her position on the dam projects and agreeing with the environmental study conducted by the legislature.

9. The stress in Holy Cross' English program is on functional writing and while teaching correct usage.

10. Privately and with sadness the friends of Alderman Jacobs feel he is embarrassing himself by supporting George Jackson's proposal.

11. In most of the wheat fields of central Illinois and where the corn grows in southern Wisconsin, the rain came and ended the worst drought in decades.

12. The upset workers got the boss' message and not liking it.

13. In May, Tau Epsilon Alpha fraternity formally decided to refurbish the old building and commissioning a local contractor to do the work.

14. This is the kind of behavior that people expect in someone else's neighborhood but not when it takes place in their own backyards.

15. Soccer fans in Tacoma not only are being attracted by the better quality of play on the part of European imports, but also those Americans playing in the league.

16. Since writing is controlled by purpose, the writer's purpose determines selection and how he organizes the content.

17. Mrs. Gavelski not only prays daily and likes going to Sunday services as an obligation but also because it offers her an opportunity to meet her friends in the Golden Agers organization.

18. What I disliked most about fishing in Ontario were the changing weather conditions and the fact that we had to drive over 19 hours to reach our destination.

19. John Enright's novel, *Watergate Reborn*, drew blistering reviews yet climbing to the best seller list and stayed there.

20. Both the manager and those who assist her were ejected from the game.

To compare: to show the likenesses or similarities between two things;
To contrast: to point out the differences between two things.

Comparison--contrast compositions are popular assignments in all academic areas. As an underclassmen in literature and English classes, you have probably compared two characters from a novel or play or contrasted yourself as a junior high student with yourself as a senior high student.

In social studies classes you might have compared the similarities between two cultures or explained the opposing viewpoints regarding a controversial political issue such as the value of the electoral college. In an art class you might have compared the styles of two famous artists such as Salvador Dali and Picasso. In a home economics class you might have compared the nutritional value of two meals.

Teachers like to assign comparison--contrast papers because these types of assignments force you not only to know the specific details of two topics but also to show the relationships of the topics being compared--contrasted.

STAGE ONE: PREWRITING

STUDENT LEARNING OBJECTIVES

1. The student will present the similarities or differences between two objects, ideas, or people.
2. The student will state the comparison and/or contrast directly in the controlling idea of the introductory paragraph.
3. The student will organize the ideas using either the block method, flip-flop method, or a combination of the two.
4. The student will include specific details and examples in the developmental paragraphs to support the controlling idea.
5. The student will use transitional words or phrases to make the topic clear for the audience (reader) to understand.
6. The student will end the composition with an effective concluding paragraph.

STUDENT MODELS

A composition developed with comparisons and contrasts presents special problems for the writer. Problem number one lies in subject selection. Often writers select two topics that are either too broad or too general. Or they choose topics that they do not have sufficient knowledge to support with concrete details. The inexperienced writer knows his first subject thoroughly but the second only superficially. His composition falls flat. He writes a classic "so what" composition.

Problem number two lies in organization. Sometimes a "shot gun blast" approach is used. The writer simply states everything she knows about both topics without carefully planning and arranging the ideas.

Before you select your own topics for this assignment, read and discuss the student model compositions.

EXERCISE 1: Use the following guide questions for each composition.

1. What is the controlling idea (thesis) in the composition? What are the two "items" being compared and/or contrasted?
2. Is the topic too broad? Does the writer have enough knowledge and information about these topics?
3. How does the introductory paragraph capture your interest? If you were writing this assignment, how would you have introduced the topic?
4. What is the writer's strategy in organizing the ideas? How would you have organized the ideas?
5. Which ideas need to be expanded to support the writer's purpose?
6. Which ideas need to be subtracted because they do not support the comparison and/or contrast?
7. How was the concluding paragraph effective?
8. What do you like **best** about the composition? What do you like **least**?
9. If you were the teacher, what would you tell the writer to improve in the composition?
10. If you were the teacher, what grade would you give the writer, assuming this was the final draft?
11. Which composition do you like **best**? Why?

Feelings

(1)   In many ways, people's attempts at covering up their feelings can be compared to a fat woman wearing a girdle.

(2)   The woman, looking in the mirror, is dismayed and appalled by what she sees. The bad muscle tone here, the roll of fat there; everything detracts from the image she wishes to present. So, the woman goes to the store and buys the strongest girdle she can find. All of the little flaws, the things she does not want anyone to see, are hidden behind the fortress of elastic.

(3)   There are problems with this, however. The girdle is uncomfortable; the flesh which has become accustomed to unrestrained freedom is suddenly compacted beyond comfort. Sometimes, the girdle does not do a very good job of hiding the imperfections. Flab spills out above and below, and when she relaxes, the poor condition of her body is still evident.

(4)   Eventually, the girdle breaks down. It cannot stand the constant strain and tension it is subjected to, and part of it weakens and gives way.

(5)   The woman goes back to the store and buys another girdle. Perhaps this one will work better than the last. She does not stop to think that perhaps it is not worth the effort.

(6)   So it is with people. We look at ourselves and are upset by what we see. The feelings of anger, envy, loathing, whatever; they all stand in the way of the image we wish to present to the world. So, we think about it for a moment, and then build the most complete facade we can muster. All of the flaws, all of the feelings we cannot admit to, all are hidden behind the formidable facade.

(7)   There are problems, however. The front we put up is uncomfortable. It does not fit. The feelings we are accustomed to expressing are suddenly restrained and hidden from view. Sometimes, the facade does not do what it is intended to do. Emotion spills out now and then, and when we relax, everything we tried to hide becomes evident.

(8)   Eventually, the facade breaks down. It cannot withhold the strain and tension of the pent-up emotions striving for expression. A piece of it weakens, and the whole thing gives way.

(9)   We go back and construct another mask to hide behind. Maybe this one will work better than the last. We never stop to think that perhaps it is not worth the effort.

Kelly and Astaire

(1) When one thinks of famous musical personalities of the 1920-50's, two names immediately come to mind, Gene Kelly and Fred Astaire. Both artists are known for their magnificent dancing skills, their top rate acting ability, and their equally impressive musical talents. They have both appeared in many of the most memorable musicals of the twentieth century. They have both taken turns working with the likes of Cyd Charisse, Judy Garland, and Leslie Caron. However, as similar as these two performers may seem, they actually differ drastically.

(2) Physically, Gene Kelly is not the "eight-by-ten glossy" type of handsome leading man, but more "the best looking guy in the neighborhood" type. He possesses an easy-going, athletic kind of grace. He is fresh and natural; his costumes are usually that of everyday street clothes.

(3) Kelly's personality suits his looks. He is very casual. These traits are reflected in his dancing. One would not picture him floating around a ballroom floor in top hat and tails. One would not imagine him waltzing about with an elegant woman in sequins and feathers. Kelly would more likely be found dancing down a street, around a barroom, or even on the deck of a ship. Some of his more unusual partners range from a cartoon mouse in *Anchors Aweigh*, to a chorus of French children in *An American in Paris*. A perfect example of Kelly's style, and perhaps his most famous dance sequence, is the scene from *Singing in the Rain*, in which he sings the title song and dances in and out of huge rain puddles on a deserted avenue. This number demonstrates his carefree, simple style.

(4) This is not to say, however, that Kelly cannot work beyond his image. Although he is noted for his casual style, he has also performed dances of the opposite extreme. The scene from *The Pirate*, in which he leaps from rooftop to rooftop, or the scene from *Summer Stock*, where he sails down a long staircase, dressed in a tuxedo, accompanied by Judy Garland, are perfect examples.

(5) Kelly, although his dances are more intellectual than they seem, makes his numbers seem unrehearsed, impromptu, as if he just suddenly had an urge to dance. He makes every step look simple and spontaneous.

(6) Fred Astaire, on the other hand, is the complete opposite of Gene Kelly. Physically, Astaire is the dignified, yet irresistibly handsome type. He is more dashing and debonair. He moves with elegance and grace. His motions are polished, flowing and graceful. Astaire's best known image is the famous "top hat, white tie, and tails" look.

(7)   Astaire, although a very sweet and humble man in real life, has most frequently played characters' possessing a cocky arrogance and boyish charm. The self-assurance and charm he has given his characters have stolen the hearts of women all over the world.

(8)   Astaire's most famous dances reflect his personality. The "Continental" from *The Gay Divorcee* or the "Cheek to Cheek" from *Top Hat* are examples of his style. Both are exquisite ballroom dances where Astaire, accompanied by Ginger Rogers, whirls around a beautiful palatial setting. He lends a dream-like quality to his movements in every step.

(9)   Astaire also displays a great amount of flexibility. Although his best known image is the classic ballroom look, he has perfectly executed routines totally opposite of this image. In contrast to his classical, ballroom dance scenes, he has danced with a drum, a chair, a coat rack, twelve pairs of feet, and up and down walls. Each was done with just as much polish as the "Carioca" or "Piccoline."

(10)   Although Gene Kelly and Fred Astaire have both emerged from the same era, and both achieved equal fame, these two men contrast each other in more ways than meets the eye. Yet as different as they are, they will both be fondly remembered as two of Hollywood's greatest dancers for years to come.

WRITING PROMPTS

Write a comparison--contrast composition about two items that have some common element, that is, they must have some component which enables them to be compared and/or contrasted. For example, playing "alley" basketball and organized high school basketball could be contrasted because of their being types of basketball. On the other hand, comparing a kayak with the luxury liner, *The Queen Mary*, as modes of water transportation would be ridiculous unless the author's purpose was to use the comparison/contrast format to write a humorous piece.

If you decide to select topics that do not seem to have any apparent common element, discuss this with your teacher for approval. The **Feelings** model on page 92 is an excellent example of a special type of comparison--contrast called an analogy. An analogy is a comparison between two normally unfamiliar objects.

Think of two objects, ideas, or people to compare and/or contrast. Possibly your topics can come from another academic area, making this a writing across the curriculum assignment.

General Topics

1 . Compare and/or contrast the teaching styles of two teachers teaching the same subject area, e.g., chemistry or physics, social studies, physical education.
2 . Compare an academic course as seen by a teacher and a student.
3 . Compare and/or contrast two sides of a current school issue: school honor code; in-school suspensions; dress code; curriculum changes, (your choice).
4 . Compare and/or contrast members of the same family: mother and father; two brothers; a brother and a sister; two grandparents.
5 . Compare and/or contrast your change in attitude towards school from freshman year to now, e.g., academics, social life, view of teachers.
6 . Compare and/or contrast the different living conditions you have encountered in your moving from the city to the suburbs, or from the country to the city, or from one part of the country to another part of the country.
7 . Compare and/or contrast two different work experiences you have had: working in a fast food restaurant such as McDonald's vs. working in an office during your summer holiday.
8 . Two television shows with the same format:
science fiction, e.g., old *Star Trek* vs. *Star Trek: The New Generation*;
crime drama, e.g., *Dragnet* vs. *NYPD BLUE*;
situation comedies, e.g., *Friends* vs. *Seinfeld*. (Your choice)

Topics from Literature

Since many of you will be using *Fan the Deck* in conjunction with your study of literature, either American, British, or World, the topic for this paper can come from something you are currently reading. Here are some ideas to get you thinking:

1 . Compare and/or contrast a character's attitudinal change in a story, novel, or play, e.g., Charlie Gordon in *Flowers for Algernon,* Bigger Thomas in *Native Son,* the young boy in "Thank You, M'am," etc.-- dynamic characters.
2 . Compare and/or contrast two characters in the literary work, e.g., the leadership qualities of Colonels Saito and Nicholson in *The Bridge over the River Kwai.*
3 . Compare and/or contrast two characters from different literary works facing a similar problem: Huck Finn from *The Adventures of Huckleberry Finn* and Holden Caulfield from *The Catcher in the R*ye.
4 . Compare and/or contrast the same theme from two different works, e.g., *The Glass Menagerie* and *A Streetcar Named Desire.*

5. Compare and/or contrast the same theme, e.g., blind acceptance of tradition; wearing someone else's shoes to understand his true feelings; social justice; honesty, etc., treated by two different novels, short stories, plays.
6. Compare two literary works by the same author, e.g., characterization in Jane Austen's *Pride and Prejudice* and *Emma*.
7. The differences between a movie version and the original play, novel, short story, e.g., "An Occurrence at Owl Creek Bridge," *Ordinary People, To Kill a Mockingbird, The Diary of Anne Frank, Romeo and Juliet* and *The West Side Story, The Color Purple,* Roman Polanski's version of *Macbeth* vs. Shakespeare's original work, Gina Berriault's "The Stone Boy."
8. Discuss other possible topics based from the literature you have already read.

Topics from Other Academic Areas

Your other academic classes could serve as another source of topics for this assignment. Before you select a topic, ask your teachers from your social studies, science, mathematics, home economics, art, music, physical education, consumer education, and computer programming classes for possible topics. Here are some writing across the curriculum topics:

Consumer Education and Home Economics

1. Become Ralph Nader for a day and write an evaluation of two products after establishing the basic criteria of evaluation.
2. Two different processes for the completion of the same goal: cooking by instinct vs. cooking by following a cookbook; *McDonalds's* vs. *Burger King*.

Computer Class

1. Comparing and/or contrasting your experiences with two different computers, e.g., Apple II C vs. Commodore; Macintosh vs. IBM PC.

Social Studies and Current Events

1. Compare and/or contrast two sides of a controversial political issue: STAR WARS; Social Security System; mandatory retirement; abortion; AIDS testing; capital punishment.
2. Compare and/or contrast the personal and political differences between two presidential candidates.

3. Compare the development of the two party system in America as reflected in the deep rooted, political, and economical differences of Alexander Hamilton and Thomas Jefferson.
4. Compare the advantages and disadvantages of both the British and American forces in the Revolutionary War.
5. Compare and/or contrast the relationship between the United States and Britain through the Jay Treaty.
6. Contrast the differences between the British view of slavery with the Spanish view of slavery.
7. Compare the presidential styles of President Clinton and President Bush or any two other presidents.
8. Contrast the role of government (specific area, e.g., Supreme Court), in people's lives in the 19th and 20th centuries. Discuss other areas as possible topics.

Physical Education

1. Compare and/or contrast two sports, e.g., soccer and football: skills required; rules; playing field.
2. If you have transferred schools, you might want to compare the physical education facilities of the two schools.

Humanities (Art and Music)

1. Compare and/or contrast the beginning of two musical forms: rock and roll, blues, jazz, etc.
2. Compare and/or contrast the styles of two artists or musicians.

Sciences and Mathematics

1. Compare and/or contrast the advantages and disadvantages of two temperature measuring devices, e.g., thermometers, optical pyrometer, etc.
2. Explain the advantages and disadvantages of expanding the nuclear power industry.
3. Compare specific types of scientists, e.g., astronomer, biologist, botanist, geochemist, geologist, geophysicists, metallurgist, physicist, zoologist.
4. Discuss the differences in various accelerators, e.g., the cyclotron, the belatron, and the synchrotron.
5. Discuss the differences between heat capacity and heat content.
6. Discuss the differences between compounds known as daltonides and bertholides.

PURPOSE AND AUDIENCE

As you begin to jot down ideas on your **Think Sheet**, consider your purpose and your audience. This will help determine the basic content of your composition. You are really asking yourself two questions. What do I want to prove in this comparison and/or contrast? Whom do I want to understand what I will be writing about?

THINK SHEET

After selecting your subject, you must think through your choices to see if you know your two items well enough to develop sufficiently. In a concrete way, your **T-Bar Think Sheet** will help you brainstorm your ideas. First, begin by listing the obvious similarities and differences of your two topics. Once you jot down one idea for the first item, jot down a corresponding idea for the second.

Do not jot down single words but phrases which illustrate a specific idea. For example, in a paper contrasting two brothers do not write:

Fred	**Sam**
responsible	*irresponsible*

but write:

Fred	**Sam**
responsible in taking out the garbage, making his bed, hanging up his clothes	*irresponsible* for he does not get up in time for school, leaves the lights on in room, and throws his clothes everywhere

List as many ideas as you can to support your comparison and/or contrast. You can always subtract the ones that do not support your thesis later.

After your **T-Bar Think Sheet** is completed, you might exchange it with a classmate. Here are some questions you might want to ask as you are examining your classmate's **T-Bar Think Sheet**.

1. Does each idea listed support the thesis of the paper?
2. What other details should be added to support the thesis? Expand.
3. Can any of the ideas be grouped to form one of the major divisions of the composition?
4. In what sequence should the grouped ideas be arranged?

Name_____

Comparison--Contrast Paper Think Sheet

1. What are the two objects, ideas, or people, etc., being compared and/or contrasted?

   A. _____

   B. _____

2. What is their common element? In other words, what do they share in that makes them topics for this assignment?

   _____

   _____

3. Who is your intended audience?_____

   _____

4. What is your purpose? What do you want to prove in this paper?

   _____

   _____

   _____

5. Using the T-bar, jot down **specific** details and examples for each item. Make it easier for yourself by listing the obvious similarities and/or differences first.

   Topic 1_____ **Topic 2**_____

   A. _____ A._____

   _____   _____

B. _____   **B.** _____

_____   _____

C. _____   **C.** _____

_____   _____

D. _____   **D.** _____

_____   _____

E. _____   **E.** _____

_____   _____

F. _____   **F.** _____

_____   _____

G. _____   **G.** _____

_____   _____

H. _____   **H.** _____

_____   _____

6. Write a tentative controlling idea (thesis), which states the two items
and indicates the direction of your paper.

_____

_____

ORGANIZING THE PAPER

If you find that you cannot list enough specific details on your **T-Bar Think Sheet** to write a sufficiently developed comparison--contrast paper, discard your **Think Sheet** and begin again. If the assignment comes from literature or some other academic area, you might have to do more research on your topic.

If you are satisfied with your **T-Bar Think Sheet**, you are ready to organize your thoughts. Break down your ideas into main divisions which will serve as the developmental paragraphs of your paper.

In organizing this "breakdown," you must decide whether you will compare, contrast, or do both. Group similar ideas and organize your divisions with a specific purpose in mind.

Block Method

One way of organizing your paper is to write all of your information on the first topic and then write all the information on the second topic. This is called the **Block Method.** This organizational pattern is used if you want the reader to see the total picture of each topic. For example, the student who wrote the **Feelings** composition on page 92 first presented all of her ideas about the problems of a woman's wearing a girdle before she pointed out the similarities with a person's feelings.

Flip-Flop Method

Another method of organization is to make one point about your first topic and then a corresponding point about the second topic. This is called the **Flip-Flop Method**. This organizational pattern is used if your purpose is to compare and/or contrast individual features of your two topics. You emphasize one specific detail of your first topic with a similar or dissimilar detail of your second.

Whichever organizational pattern you select, make sure that you cover the same points for each subject. You can also use a combination of these organizational patterns.

COHERENCE (GLUING TOGETHER IDEAS)

In writing a **comparison--contrast paper**, use transition words to make the points of your comparison and/or contrast clear to your reader. One method is by using transition words that show similarities or that point out differences.

Transition words for similarities: similarly, likewise, in the same manner, in a similar fashion, again, also, another, besides, for example, furthermore, in addition, moreover, too.

Transition words for differences: although, as if, but, even if, however, in spite of, nevertheless, on the other hand, otherwise, still, yet.

As a quick review, note the transitional words and phrases used in the **Kelly and Astaire** composition on pages 93-94.

Another way of gluing together ideas is to repeat similar sentence patterns or to repeat key phrases. This not only links ideas but also creates impact through the repetition of key words. The **Feelings** model is an excellent example of the use of repeated structures.

INTRODUCTORY AND CONCLUDING PARAGRAPHS

The choice of what type of introductory and concluding paragraphs you will write and whether you write them before or after writing the developmental paragraphs is up to you. Here is a list of the sample introductory and concluding paragraphs included in *Fan the Deck*:

Introductory Paragraphs

Background Information, pages 51, 76
Definition, 17, 50
Direct Statement of Fact, 49, 76
Example or Illustration, 50
Exploration of Known Ideas, 51
Incident, 17, 141
Negation, 17
Question, 17
Quotation, 52
Startling Statement, 140

Concluding Paragraphs

Emotional Appeal, page 142
Proposition Restated as a Conclusion, 18, 77
Quotation, 52
Sense of Finality, 77
Subject's Importance, 18, 142
Summarization, 53, 77

STAGE TWO: WRITING THE FIRST DRAFT

For many students writing the first draft is the most crucial part of the assignment. Do not be concerned with mechanical and grammatical errors. Concentrate on including everything you want incorporated in the paper. Use your **T-Bar Think Sheet** to help you remember your main points.

Here is a summary of some of the main objectives:

1. Capture your reader's interest in your introduction. Make sure your audience knows the two subjects that you are comparing and/or contrasting and your purpose.
2. If you want your reader to see a separate picture of each subject, organize your ideas using the **Block Method**.
3. If you want your reader to see the individual features of each topic, organize your ideas using the **Flip-Flop Method**.
4. If you want to emphasize some individual features and some total picture, use a combination of both methods.
5. Use transition words to make the relationship of your ideas easier for your reader to understand.
6. Support both topics with specific details.
7. End with a sense of finality.

Now write your first draft.

STAGE THREE: REWRITING

SENTENCE OPENING SHEET

After you have written your first draft including your introductory and concluding paragraphs, fill out the **Sentence Opening Sheet** as directed by your teacher. For many of you, filling out the **Sentence Opening Sheet** can be omitted at this time if you have already spotted the errors the **SOS Sheet** helps identify. This is with teacher approval, of course.

See pages 18-20 for an explanation of the **SOS Sheet**.

PEER EVALUATION USING A CHECKLIST SHEET

In the prewriting stage you selected two topics and listed your ideas using the **T-Bar Think Sheet**. In the writing stage you decided on the basic content and organized your ideas with a specific purpose in mind.

In the rewriting stage you must concentrate on tightening up your organization and making sure that each detail in your developmental paragraphs supports the thesis or controlling idea of your introductory paragraph.

Now, read your first draft aloud and then ask yourself the following questions:

1. Can someone listening to me read my composition aloud identify my controlling idea? Is the purpose of my composition clearly stated in the controlling idea (thesis)?
2. In listening to me read my composition, could my listener identify my overall organization? Would she be able to tell that I used the **Block Method**, **Flip-Flop Method**, or combination?
3. Which specific details or examples present similarities or point out differences?
4. Do I have balance to my subjects? In other words, if I stressed one point about my first topic did I include a corresponding idea for the second topic?
5. Do I need to expand to make my supportive ideas clearer for the reader?
6. Do I need to subtract any ideas that do not support my controlling idea?
7. Do my transition words make it easier for my listener to understand the relationships of my ideas?
8. Is my ending effective or does it fall flat?

Writer's Name_____

Evaluator's Name_____

Comparison-Contrast Checklist

Introductory Paragraph

1. What are the two subjects being compared and/or contrasted?

2. How did the introductory paragraph capture your interest?

Developmental Paragraphs

3. How does each developmental paragraph contribute to the paper's overall purpose?

4. How did the writer organize his ideas?

5. Mark the transition words or repeated phrases used to make the connection between the paragraphs smooth.

Concluding Paragraph

6. Identify the type of concluding paragraph.

7. How does the concluding paragraph suggest finality?

Style and Mechanics

8. Correct any mistakes, including spelling and punctuation errors.

9. What did you like best about this paper?

FINAL COPY AFTER PEER EVALUATION

Follow the same procedure that you have been using as you prepare your final copy. Undoubtedly, you are editing your final draft based on your reading the paper aloud three or four times. You are probably becoming an expert in identifying and correcting common sentence errors.

Your final draft should be neat and error-free, a model of your finest writing. It should be something that you are proud to submit to your teacher.

STAGE FOUR: PUBLISHING

A comparison-contrast paper is an ideal one for an oral report or speech.

Also, if some classmates have written on similar topics, e.g., products, environmental issues, you might want to compile your essays in a book format. Or you might want to exchange papers to see how they handle the same topics.

Finally, you might want to include your paper in a writing portfolio.

If you plan to attend college, or even if you apply for a job, sooner or later you will have to write a letter of application. Almost always the instructions for writing the letter asks you to tell about yourself, your activities, and your interests.

Often the instructions also ask you to include something about your special qualities. Usually it is easy to include something about your interests, but writing about yourself and your special qualities can cause the most dreaded of all diseases: **Brain Lock!** The problem is how to present yourself well without sounding like the biggest braggart since the world began.

Before you panic, before you decide to forego college or a job, before you decide to become a hermit, try using this unit to help you write that winning personal letter of application.

STAGE ONE: PREWRITING

STUDENT LEARNING OBJECTIVES

1. The student will write a letter of application to a college or for a job.
2. The student will include the six parts of a business letter: heading, address, greeting, body, closing, and signature.
3. The student will tell about his special interests and activities in a way that demonstrate orderly thinking.
4. The student will reveal a special quality by using specific details to describe a personal anecdote or reflection.
5. The student will use vivid verbs and appropriate transitions to add color and coherence to the letter.
6. The student will use first person point of view without shifting to second person reference, i.e., "you."
7. The student will use a tone appropriate to his subject matter.

In an English class, criticism is the act of examining and judging the comparative worth of a literary work. When a letter requesting admission to a university is submitted by an applicant, that letter is carefully *criticized* by an admissions office "judge."

The admissions office is charged with judging which applicants are worthy of admission to the school. Obviously the admissions "judge" will examine and evaluate each letter of application very seriously.

Since many more students submit letters of application than will be accepted at the college, the admissions office often determines who will be selected based on the letter. Therefore, a good letter of application is definitely an asset if a student wishes to be considered for admission to the university or college of his choice.

Usually the admissions officer will be looking for two factors: 1) what kind of person the applicant is; and 2) whether or not the applicant writes clearly.

In evaluating the letter, an admissions officer must determine whether or not the writer answered the questions which were asked in the application form. It is important, then, that the applicant carefully analyzes the questions to be sure that he is on the right track when he writes his responses.

Another criteria that the officer considers is the letter itself. Certainly the writer will need to avoid vague, general responses. Instead, the writer must use specific examples which give the reader an overall view of what he is like.

In short, the admissions officer wants to find out if the applicant can write. That is what this unit is all about: how to make a good impression through clear, specific answers which reveal your "wonderfulness" without making you sound like North America's #1 hot air balloon.

CRITIQUING A COLLEGE ADMISSION LETTER

EXERCISE 1: Play the role of a college admissions officer as you read the following letter of application. Remember that you are looking for two main things:

1. What kind of person wrote this letter?
2. Did the writer express himself clearly?

9568 Welsch Road
Winneconne, Wisconsin 54986
November 24, 2003

Dean of Admissions
Harvard - Radcliffe
Office of Admissions and Financial Aid
Byerly Hall, 8 Garden Street
Cambridge, MA 02138

Dear Ms. Addie Mission:

I would like to come to your school, Harvard University. I am graduating this spring from Valley West High School with the rank of eleventh in my class of 456. My grade point average is 3.73. I want to come to Harvard on account of the fact that I think I will like it there, and I will be able to learn many things so that I can be successful in my chosen career of business. After all, Harvard is rated as the best university in America. Everybody says so. And it has a very fine business school.

I have had an extremely active high school experience. I have been part of the Academic Challenge team. We placed third in state competition with twenty-four teams. I personally received an award for having participated on the team for the greatest length of time, since I was a freshman. Also, I am a member of the National Honor Society. I am the coordinator for the tutoring program. Also, I do many hours of tutoring myself. I have worked extremely hard to achieve an excellent academic record as you can see by my grade point average and class rank.

In addition, I have been very active in extra-curricular activities. I have been in track for the last four years. The last two as a member of the varsity team. I ran the high hurdles and jumped the high jump and the triple jump. Last year I won the district title for the high jump and took second in the triple jump. I went to state with three other members of my team where I came in sixth in the high jump and fifteenth in the triple jump.

Also, I played basketball during the four years of my high school career. I was chosen the member of the team to receive the Steadiest Player Award at the end of last season. I also participate in the Spanish Club, where I am the vice-president, and the National Junior Science and Humanities Symposium. Last year I was awarded the place of alternate for the national competition. This spring I hope to get the number one position in state, so that I can go to the national competition in Walla Walla, Washington. Music is another of my activities, and I am a member of the Concert Band. I often perform as soloist on my flute, and I have been awarded a Certificate of Excellence for my fine playing by the Music Adjudicators' Conference held each winter for the last three conferences.

109

I have led an active life outside the school in the community. I am a member of the Conference of Youth at my church. I am active in the Boy Scouts of America. I participate as a member of the high school age troop, and I assist as the assistant leader of a troop of elementary age boys. I donate my time and talent to play my flute once a month at the local nursing home for retired senior citizens.

I have many interests and hobbies of my own. I like to read about science, both fiction and non-fiction. I like to play handball with my brother or my father. I like to ride my bicycle in bike-a-thons with some of my friends. I like video games, and I like to spend time composing short stories on my personal computer, a Macintosh Plus with a 20 megabyte internal hard drive.

I plan a career in business as I said previously. I will get a B. S. degree first, then try to get accepted into Harvard's prestigious graduate school to receive my Masters of Business Administration degree. After that, I will work in the office of some famous company in New York. Attending Harvard will help me to achieve this goal on account of the fact the Harvard graduate gets hired easily in the business world and make lots of money.
I thank you for the opportunity to apply for admission to Harvard. I hope you will find my humble record worthy of your attention. I believe my meager accomplishments will lead you to accept me to your university. I shall be waiting to hear from you soon.

Sincerely yours,

Norman Konquest

EXERCISE 2: After reading Norman's letter, answer the following questions. Remember that as an admissions officer, you are trying to decide if Norman would benefit from attending your university as well as whether he would fit into it.

1 . First, rank the letter on a scale of 1 to 10 for its warmth and appeal. Suggestions: Give it a "10" if you want to meet Norman immediately because you are sure that he will become the President by the time he is forty-three. Give it a "5" if Norman sounds like a nice guy even if he is a little boring. Give it a "1" if you feel like throwing it in the trash compactor.

2. Next, analyze the letter to see why it made you react the way you did. Find specific examples in the letter to answer the questions below.
What **kind of a person** wrote the letter?

a. What positive aspects about Norman impressed you?
b. What negative things did you notice?
c. Is Norman a responsible, effective student? Why or why not?
d. What is Norman's personality like? How is it revealed?
e. What are his reasons for choosing Harvard?
f. If you did not like Norman, why? What words did he use to form your opinion?

Is Norman an **effective writer**?

a. Were you able to read and understand the letter easily?
b. Is the letter clearly organized? Is anything out of place?
c. Are the supporting details specific and interesting? Are the details listed in a "ho-hum" manner?
d. Is there variety in sentence lengths, openings, and patterns?
e. Are the words carefully chosen for their exact meaning? Are some words overused or dull?
f. Are there any misspelled words, misplaced commas, etc.?
g. Did Norman use any trite expressions?

Compare notes with a classmate. You may even want to do the whole exercise with a partner(s). Just remember to be kind to Norman--it could be **YOU!**

After analyzing the letter thoroughly both for content and for writing, you are ready to make a judgment. Finally, the big question:

Will you admit Norman Konquest to Harvard? Why or why not?

WRITER'S SUBJECT, AUDIENCE, AND PURPOSE

For this particular assignment, it is remarkably easy to identify both subject and audience. You are the **subject**, and the college admissions officer is the **audience**. All you have to do is decide how to achieve your **purpose**: gaining admission to the college of your choice. You have to decide how to impress the admissions officer favorably. You must determine what information to include and what will give your letter warmth and appeal.

TONE

You must also establish a specific tone in your letter. Tone is the feeling created by the way words and sentences are used by the writer. Deciding how you want your reader to feel will help you choose which words and sentence patterns to use.

If you did not like Norman, he must have used words that formed your opinion of him. He created an arrogant tone. You want to be positive in your letter. For more explanation of the meaning of tone, read page 143 in the **Argumentative Paper** unit.

THINK SHEET

Before you write your first draft, brainstorm on a **Think Sheet** just as you have done for the other assignments in *Fan the Deck*. For this assignment a **Think Sheet** will be especially helpful. It will give you an opportunity to think about yourself and all your accomplishments. Even if you are only a sophomore or a junior, this will enable you to practice for your senior year.

If the college or university to which you are applying has a special application form, you might want to use that form for your brainstorming.

Complete the **Think Sheet** as fully as you can. Do not list only "dry" details. Use unusual items which reveal the real *you*. Select items from the **Think Sheet** that best reflect your values and the type of person you are when you write your first draft.

You will probably choose not to use everything you list on your **Think Sheet** in your letter, but having many details to choose from will be about the most helpful thing you can do to write a successful letter. In fact, the **Think Sheet** will probably be considerably longer than the finished letter.

Keep the admissions officer's two main questions in mind as you write:

1. What type of person is the applicant?
2. Does he write clearly?

Name_____

College Application Think Sheet

1. Intended College_____

2. My Purpose_____

_____

_____

3. Tone_____

4. Goals and plans I have for the future. (You do not have to know an exact career you want. Instead, consider what you think will be your priorities for life.) Why have I chosen these goals?

    A.   When and Why I decided to go to college in the first place. Be specific.

        _____

        _____

    B.   Reasons why I want to attend this particular college. List several.

        _____

        _____

    C.   Reasons why I would be an asset to this college. List several.

        _____

        _____

    D.   High school activities. Include sports, service organizations, special interest clubs, student government.

        _____

        _____

E.   Awards, honors, or special recognition.

_____

_____

F.   Non-school activities: include church, community, service
organizations.

_____

_____

G.   Fun and relaxation: interests, hobbies, likes, dislikes, good books.

_____

_____

H.   Work experiences: baby-sitting, berry picking, fast food restaurants.

_____

_____

I.   Other: travel, unusual experiences, special circumstances, health.

_____

_____

J.   Personal qualities: strengths, attitudes, skills, talents.

_____

_____

K.   A short history of myself. Ancestors count, too!_____

L. Person I most admire. Why?_____

_____

_____

_____

M. Little known facts about myself. (Something that makes me different from any of my friends. For example: I was born on February 29th. My grandfather was a soldier in World War II. I raise Burmese cats.)

_____

_____

_____

_____

N. How I would change the world, or what I think the world will be like in the year 2010.

_____

_____

_____

_____

5. Tentative Controlling Idea_____

_____

_____

_____

CONTROLLING IDEA AND PURPOSE

A letter of application must have a controlling idea just as any other paper. Often, though, the idea is not written in a thesis statement in the letter. The writer simply puts the controlling idea on the **Think Sheet** and uses it to guide the items and details which he includes in the letter.

Remember that the controlling idea should be a clear statement of the important points you want to make. It should also give some indication of the effect you want to create, that is, how you want the reader to feel about you.

Here are some examples of controlling ideas:

Example: I will make a good college student because I am hard-working, responsible, and friendly.

Example: Going to college is important for me to become the person I want to be: knowledgeable, observant, caring, active, involved, wealthy, and witty!

ORGANIZING THE LETTER

Decide how you will organize the letter. You may want to follow the format suggested in the application form. If the form does not include a format, then you will need to determine how you are going to present yourself in the letter. Following are some suggestions to help you decide.

Chronological Order

If the application directions ask for any of your history or autobiography, one way to organize would be in a time sequence. Of course, you would want to avoid any statement like, "I was born . . . " (Most people were, you know!) That opening is an automatic signal that this letter will be boooooring.

The "Block" Method

The "Block" organizes items of like-natures into blocks. For instance, you organize your athletic participation into one block, your community experiences in another block, your hobbies and interests in still another block, and so on. Then you arrange the blocks according to how you think they best demonstrate orderly thinking. Here you are almost ready for college and still playing with blocks!

Year by Year Order

One clear way to organize the essay is to relate your activities and experiences each year that you have been in high school. First, you tell all you can about your freshman year, then your sophomore year, and so on. You should be careful to organize the items in the same sequence each time. If activities are first and sports are second in the first paragraph, then the same order should be followed in the second paragraph, and so on.

Remember to use appropriate transitions to provide coherence for the reader.

Transitions: furthermore, in addition, also, at the time, for example, throughout, according to, when, even though, because, as a result of, whenever, after, etc.

BLOCK LETTER FORM

The Block Letter Form is perhaps the easiest and best way to set up a letter of application. There are six parts to this form: heading, inside address, greeting, body, complimentary closing, and signature.

Heading: The writer's complete mailing or return address. It is placed at least one and one-half inches from the top of the paper. The date is immediately below the address. The month should be spelled out, not abbreviated.

Examples:

8301 Pleasant Avenue	16842 New Buffalo
Los Angeles, CA 99201	Tinley Park, IL 60477
January 22, 2002	September 10, 2003

Inside Address: The inside address includes the name of the person you are writing to and the complete address. A person's name in the inside address should be prefaced with a courtesy title such as Mr., Mrs., or Ms. If you know the official title of the person, put the title after the name or below the name.

Examples:

Mrs. Letta Emmin, Dean	Dr. Dean College
New Student Office	Admissions Officer
Carnegie-Mellon University	University of Oregon
5115 Margaret Morrison St.	P. O. Box 2373
Pittsburgh, PA 15213	Eugene, OR 97403

Here is an example of an inside address when the name is not known:

Admissions Office
University of Southern California
1503 Hoover Boulevard
Los Angeles, CA 90089-0018

Salutation or Greeting: The salutation is a greeting. It is always followed by a colon. When the name of the person is known, you should use these greetings: Dear Mrs. Emmin:, Dear Dr. College:.

When writing to an individual whose name is not known, use Dear Sir: or Dear Madam:.

Body: The body is the most important part of the letter. Here you state your message in a clear and direct manner. The tone of your application should be pleasant, direct, and courteous. A *Please* and *Thank you* attitude goes a long way.

Complimentary Close: The complimentary close indicates the closing of the letter. Typical closings are **Sincerely yours,** or **Yours truly,**. Notice that the first word is capitalized and the last word is followed by a comma. (**HINT**: Be especially careful of the spelling of these words. They are all too often misspelled, and you do not want to leave a bad impression!)

Signature: The last basic part of the letter is the signature. The choice of including your middle name or initial is yours. You should use the signature that you would write in any business transaction.

Your letter should be typewritten, unless the application form specifically asks you to handwrite it. Your signature should be handwritten between the complimentary close and your typewritten name. Remember there is nothing particularly admirable about a signature that cannot be read, so write your name clearly and proudly.

GOOD MODEL

Finally, before you begin to write the first draft of your most amazing letter ever, here is a good model to inspire you. Read it and enjoy it. This letter not only earned the writer admission to the college of her choice but also a substantial amount of scholarship money. Notice especially the warm, appealing tone of her letter. Look it over carefully to see what Staci Ness did to achieve that tone.

2811 East Eleventh Avenue
Spokane, Washington 99202
January 30, 2004

Admissions Office
University of Washington
400 15th Avenue NE
Seattle, Washington 98105

Dear Dean Whithim:

I woke up one morning in a cold sweat. I had been having a nightmare. It was my first year of teaching and I was drowning in a sea of freshmen compositions. Once awake with my feet firmly planted in the "real" world, I asked myself why I wanted to be part of a profession reputedly plagued by low pay, disrespectful students, and uninvolved parents.
I suppose it all started when I was a first grader. I would come home from school, get out my little chalkboard, and force my three-year-old brother to listen to the basic principles of addition and subtraction. And although he was much less than the ideal student, I still knew at the all-experienced age of six that a teacher was what I would be when I grew up.

Somehow, that goal never changed. Like other children, I went through the stages of wanting to become a firewoman, a detective, an airline stewardess, but my original plan remained the same. My biggest dilemma was what to teach. The answer was revealed to me by my eighth grade teacher, Mr. Holmes, my English teacher. He taught me that there was much more to English than grammar, mechanics, and reading. He opened the world of interpretation, poetry, writing, Shakespeare, and Dickens. It was then that I decided to teach English.

There was another teacher, also, one who added more depth to my perception of teaching. I learned from Miss Snowden that teaching did not only involve subject matter but also involved the sculpting of lives to create young adults who had self-esteem and confidence, who believed they could be anything or anybody they wanted. I decided I wanted to accept the challenge.

119

I plunged into high school with enthusiasm. I joined athletics: the volleyball team, the basketball team, the softball team. I joined the Spanish Club and the Students Against Drunk Drivers (SADD) organization, and was named to the National Honor Society as a sophomore. I participated in the drama productions and in the student government. I was honored to receive the "Most Valuable Player" award for volleyball and the "Most Inspirational" award for softball. I liked being the secretary of the Spanish Club and the president of SADD. I kept busy with my studies and my high school activities, but I also enjoyed singing with the Zion Lutheran Youth Choir, working part time at the local pizza take-out, and reading in my spare time.

Life is fun sometimes and sometimes hard, but it is always challenging. I have confidence that I can reach my goal of being a successful teacher, but I know that I will need all the help and support that I can find. That is why I chose the University of Washington School of Education for my college. I feel sure that is where I will receive the background I need to make English exciting and rewarding for my future students. Furthermore, I expect to find the type of role model that I wish to become. I look for people in my life whom I can respect, and I strive to learn what makes them such fine people. I ask questions, and I thoughtfully think over my answers. I hope that my awareness of good role models will help me to become one. I will make mistakes. Mr. Holmes and Miss Snowden did too, but, like them, I can learn from my mistakes and do better the next time.

I am sure there will be more nightmares. But they will not change my mind. Somewhere inside me there will always be that little girl with the chalkboard.

Sincerely yours,

Staci Ness

Staci Ness

STAGE TWO: WRITING THE FIRST DRAFT

You have completed the **Think Sheet** with its controlling idea in front of you. Now is the time to write that winning letter.

Be sure that your introduction is a "catcher." If your letter does not interest the admissions officer immediately, your chances at the college of your dreams may never materialize!

Remember to write in first person without slipping into second person "you." Use specific details to personalize what you write. The reader is not interested in a list of dry statistics. Use vivid, concrete verbs to add color and action.

Now write your letter.

STAGE THREE: REWRITING

SENTENCE OPENING SHEET

After you have completed a first draft, you will want to self-analyze your writing to make sure you have the best possible letter. Use the **Sentence Opening Sheet** and the **Student Objectives and Evaluation Sheet** your teacher distributed in the prewriting stage as your guide.

PEER EVALUATION USING A CHECKLIST SHEET

If your teacher does not pair you off with a partner or put you in a support group, find someone who will give you an honest opinion of your letter. Perhaps your boyfriend or girlfriend, your guidance counselor, your parents, or a friend who is particularly good at writing would be a good choice. The person who critiques the letter for you may find the questions following the poor model (remember Norman?) helpful as a guide for criticism of your letter. You may also use the **Checklist Sheet** on the next page.

Applicant's Name_____

Evaluator's Name_____

College Application Checklist

Directions: Pretend that you are an admissions officer and evaluate your partner's paper. Be honest.

1. What information did the applicant include so that you know the type of person he is?

2. In writing about his interests and activities, how was the applicant specific or did he write in vague generalities, simply listing his accomplishments?

3. Based on the information in the letter, what special qualities does the applicant possess that would make him a valuable member of next year's incoming freshman class?

4. What reasons did the applicant give for wanting to attend the desired school? Were the reasons legitimate or just a series of trite, ballooned expressions?

5. How did the applicant organize his letter?

6. How did the letter move smoothly from paragraph to paragraph, demonstrating coherence or was it just a hodge-podge of ideas thrown together?

7. How does the applicant adhere to the same guidelines for this letter as he would for any other composition: variety in sentence openings and lengths, consistent point of view, strong verbs, good word choice, etc.?

8. Check to see that the letter adheres to the guidelines of the block format.

9. As an admissions officer, why would you admit the applicant?

10. As an admissions officer, why would you **not** admit the applicant?

FINAL LETTER AFTER PEER EVALUATION

After your letter has been criticized and revised, type the final draft. Before you place your masterpiece in an appropriately addressed envelope and off to the "judges," reread it three or four times aloud, concentrating on one objective per reading.

Make your letter perfect. It could have a great impact upon your next four years. Good Luck!

STAGE FOUR: PUBLISHING

Before you send your letter to the colleges of your choice, some volunteers might read their letters to the class. Or you might have your college counselor check over your application letter.

Also, your letter might be a good selection for your writing portfolio.

In the **Parallelism** unit you combined equal ideas with equal structures. You used coordinating and correlative conjunctions. You also coordinated by writing sentences with compound verbs, compound verbals, and relative clauses. Now you will combine and rearrange ideas, but instead of making ideas equal, you will be emphasizing important ideas and **subordinating** less important ideas.

SUBORDINATION IN WRITING

In a simple sentence one main idea is stressed. In a compound sentence two or more equal ideas are stressed. Each idea is a complete thought by itself.

Simple Sentences: Kerrie lost her starting position on the volleyball team. She remained loyal to the team despite her diminished role.

Compound Sentence: Kerrie lost her starting position on the volleyball team, **but** she remained loyal to the team despite her diminished role.

In the compound sentence above, the two main ideas are of equal importance because both of them are complete thoughts. However, if one of the main thoughts was more important, you would need to subordinate the lesser idea. This enables you to make the relationship of ideas clear. It also enables you to subtract unnecessary words or ideas.

In the following examples the subordinated ideas have been italicized.

ING Phrase: *Despite los**ing** her starting position on the volleyball team,* Kerrie remained loyal in her diminished role.

Past Participle: *Disappoint**ed** by the loss of her starting position on the volleyball team,* Kerrie remained loyal despite her diminished role.

Relative Clause: Kerrie, ***who** was once a starter on the volleyball team,* has remained loyal despite her diminished role.

Appositive: Kerrie, *a one-time **starter** on the volleyball team,* remained loyal despite her diminished role.

Subordinating Conjunction:	**Although** Kerrie lost her starting job on the volleyball team, she remained loyal to the team despite her diminished role.

Subordination, then, is emphasizing a main idea by writing it in an independent clause and **subordinating** lesser ideas by writing them in dependent clauses or phrases. The subordinate idea is not a complete sentence. It is a fragment.

USING ING PHRASES AND PAST PARTICIPLES TO SUBORDINATE LESSER IDEAS

One way of emphasizing a main idea is to subordinate the lesser idea by expressing it in an ING phrase, either a present participle or a gerund. Since present participles and gerunds end in *ING*, we have called them ING words throughout the *Stack the Deck* writing series.

In revising a composition, you want to make sure that you do not join unequal ideas in a compound sentence. You can subordinate by combining and rearranging the ideas correctly.

Mrs. Weinberg was looking unhappy, and she walked into the school cafeteria.

The present participle is the *ING* form of the verb used as an adjective.

Looking unhappy, Mrs. Weinberg walked into the school cafeteria.

In the previous example, the writer subordinated by using an ING phrase. The main idea in the sentence is that *Mrs. Weinberg walked into the school cafeteria.* However, if the writer wanted to emphasize Mrs. Weinberg's looking unhappy, he could have written the following ING participial phrase.

Walking into the school cafeteria, Mrs. Weinberg looked unhappy.

The main idea should always be a complete sentence by itself.

The past participle form of the verb (ED word) also subordinates lesser ideas. Note how the writer subordinated the lesser idea in the following sentence by using an ED phrase.

125

Example: My dad was disturbed by the kids' talking during the movie, and my dad complained to the manager of the theater.

Revised: **Disturbed** *by the kids' talking during the movie,* my dad complained to the theater's manager.

or

My dad, **disturbed** *by the kids' talking during the movie,* complained to the theater's manager.

EXERCISE 1: Combine and rearrange the following set of sentences, using ING phrases and/or ED phrases to subordinate lesser ideas. The most important idea should receive the most emphasis. You can write your responses in more than one sentence.

Example: I failed the exam miserably, and I consulted with my physics teacher after the class, and I found out that I had inadvertently forgotten to answer all the questions on the exam.

Revised: I failed the physics exam miserably. **After consulting with my physics teacher**, I found out that I had inadvertently forgotten to answer all the questions on the exam. (The writer used two sentences.)

1. Chauncey Albright ran down the hall, and Chauncey banged into an open locker door, and he broke his glasses.
2. The puppies were frightened by the crash of thunder, and they hid under the blankets.
3. The video camera panned the discussion. The video camera focused on the moderator of the program.
4. The old witch doctor stuck pins in the voodoo doll. He hoped this would bring harm to the intruders.
5. Mayor Joan Burn hoped to suppress the negative publicity, and at the same time she wished to encourage good press relations, and she organized a dinner for members of the press corp.
6. Dr. Josephine Malinskis hoped to stop the bleeding. She cut out six inches of the main artery. She had the patient prepped for emergency surgery.
7. I was left alone in the cottage during the tornado, and I huddled in the shower stall with blankets and pillows all over me.
8. Carla listened to her father's and mother's opinions, and she began to form her own opinion on the topic.
9. Scott was intrigued by his dad's comment. He decided to study the matter more closely.
10. The chicken was made with a peanut sauce. It is one of my favorite recipes.

126

USING RELATIVE PRONOUNS AND APPOSITIVES TO SUBORDINATE LESSER IDEAS

Relative pronouns "relate" dependent clauses to main clauses. They show how a dependent clause describes an independent clause. Since most relative pronouns begin with *WH,* we have called them WH words throughout our series. Here is a list of relative pronouns (WH words):

who, whom, whose, which and **that**
Note the one exception to the rule, *that.*

In revising sentences, you can subordinate by placing the less important idea in a relative clause introduced by the WH word.

Sentence: Chick Simpson parked in front of the fire plug, and he received a fifteen dollar ticket and the infamous Denver boot.

Relative   Chick Simpson **who parked in front of the fire plug**
Clause: received a fifteen dollar ticket and the infamous Denver boot.

Special Punctuation Rule: Commas are used to punctuate nonrestrictive clauses, that is, clauses that are not necessary to the meaning of the sentence. If you can subtract the clause and the meaning of your sentence does not change, then the clause is nonrestrictive.

An **appositive** is a word or phrase that comes directly after a noun or pronoun and provides additional information. It renames or explains the noun or pronoun.

Example: Zelda Zigmundski, the author of *Little Ben's Revenge,* has been named the Illinois Writer of the Year by the state English teachers association.

The phrase *the author of Little Ben's Revenge* provides additional information about Zelda Zigmundski.

An appositive is another way of subordinating.

Example: Gwen Symth is the winner of the Kane County Apple Pie Bakeoff, and she used apples laced with grapefruit juice.

Appositive: Gwen Symth, *the winner of the Kane County Apple Pie Bakeoff,* used apples laced with grapefruit juice.

Special Punctuation Rule: If the appositive provides extra information, it is set off by commas. However, if it is essential information, no commas are necessary.

- Mr. Barrett, *a distinguished looking white-haired gentleman*, owns a construction company. (Commas needed.)
- The lineman *Horatio Simmons* was the first Brother Rice High School player to receive a football scholarship to Oklahoma University. (No commas needed.)

EXERCISE 2: Combine the following sentences, using relative pronouns and appositive phrases to subordinate lesser ideas. Write each sentence two ways. The main idea should always be the complete sentence.

1. Mick E. Loebb has a very strict security system at Bush Stadium. He owns the St. Louis Bombers. He controls the world's largest horse farm.

2. Seattle has a very mild climate, and it is the gateway to the orient, and it is the home of Jake O'Shaughnessey's, and Jake O'Shaughnessey's serves the best prime rib dinner in Seattle.

3. Tracey Caustin won the Colgate Tennis Championship, and she is only 17 years old, and she is a student at Sammamish High School.

4. Tic Toc Ltd. produces one-half of the computerized watches used by the United States Air Force. Tic Toc Ltd. was formerly a manufacturer of telephone equipment. Tic Toc Ltd. grossed $330, 000, 000 last year.

5. Dr. Mona Lott authored three books on the judiciary system, and she was the president of Lake Shore University, and she was appointed Undersecretary of Internal Security.

6. The photograph showed the little baby holding a lion cub. The photo won first prize.

7. *Othello* is a play about jealousy. *Othello* is one of William Shakespeare's most famous tragedies. *Othello* is seldom taught in high school.

8. Frank Capra is the director of *It's a Wonderful Life.* Frank Capra loved to glorify the common man in his movies.

9. Nelson Fox played second base for the Chicago White Sox in 1959. Nelson Fox was my boyhood idol.

10. *The Old Man and the Sea* is a novel about the ordeal of an old Cuban fisherman. It is one of Ernest Hemingway's finest novels.

USING SUBORDINATING CONJUNCTIONS TO SUBORDINATE LESSER IDEAS

A subordinate clause is a group of words with a subject and a verb that cannot stand by itself. It is dependent upon the main clause to make sense. It is introduced by a subordinating conjunction, which *glues* the subordinate clause to the main clause. In other **Stack the Deck, Inc.** textbooks we have referred to subordinating conjunctions as glue words because of their function.

- *Although* Judge Wappner answered the defendant's question.
- *Because* the Alonzo received $3,000,000 in TV commercial money his first year in the National Football League.
- *Wherever* I feel like going.
- *In order that* Ernie be given a clean slate.
- *As long as* the residents are still concerned about a quality education for their children.
- *If* you will not help me fix the flat tire.

Using a subordinate clause is another way of subordinating. The main idea that you want to emphasize is a complete thought by itself. The lesser idea is written as a subordinate clause. The subordinating conjunction indicates the relationship of ideas. Here is a listing of subordinating conjunctions:

Subordinating Conjunctions	Relationship
Although, even though, though, even if, while	Concession (yielding: granting an opposing point)
Because, since, so that, as	Cause
If, unless	Condition
Where, wherever	Place
In order that, that, so that	Purpose
As a result, so that	Result
When, whenever, while, until, before as long as, as soon as, since, as, after	Time

EXERCISE 3: Rewrite the following sentences, emphasizing the most important idea in the main clause and lesser idea in the subordinate clause. Use the subordinating conjunctions listed above.

Example: E. J. Molitor stayed on the interstate, and the interstate was crowded with rush hour traffic.

Revised: <u>Even though the interstate was crowded with rush hour traffic,</u> E. J. Molitor stayed on it.

> **Special Punctuation Rule:** If a subordinate clause comes at the beginning of a sentence, separate it from the main clause by a comma. If the subordinate clause comes after the main clause, a comma is not normally needed.
>
> *If you will help me solve the trig problem,* I will treat you to a chocolate malt.
> I will treat you to a chocolate malt *if you help me solve the trig problem.*

1. Joshua Arnold performed well at rehearsals, and he was selected to play Scrooge in Dickens' *The Christmas Carol.*
2. Theresa Gingers is a "Cover Girl" model, and she works at national conventions, and she introduces the latest fashions.
3. Emil Sovada started growing asparagus in California. All local stores purchased this vegetable from his business.
4. Maz Cahill has been practicing figure dancing for ten years. She was not named to the Irish Olympic team.
5. The Secretary of the Navy disagreed with the President's budget cuts, and she resigned.
6. The federal meat inspectors visit the cutting room every day, and the Prince Meat Company sells only the finest meat.
7. Dr. Maria Lopez Conchis performed emergency surgery. Harvey Degutis will not be able to play soccer again.
8. Ezekiel Mahoney lost his temper, and the news of his candidacy was prematurely released on television.
9. The king-makers manipulated the funds illegally, and the real estate deal involving millions fell through.
10. The classical concept of education is being threatened, and the advances of technology demand more and more specialization.

EXERCISE 4: Rewrite the following sentences, emphasizing the most important idea in the main clause and subordinating the lesser idea in a dependent clause. You can write your answers in more than one sentence.

Example:　　Bucky Bates plays "Monopoly." He should open the box. He should spread out the board. He should count the money. He should check the cards.

Revised:　　Before Bucky Bates plays "Monopoly," he should spread out the board, count the money, and check the cards.

1. Robin Budz steps up to the free throw line, and she takes the ball from the referee, and she prepares herself mentally, and she bounces the ball three times. The ball leaves her finger-tips. She maintains a lingering control. The ball plunges into the core of the basket. The roar of the fans erupts.

2. Police Officer Annette Buday felt a surge of satisfaction, and she made her first arrest.

3. Dwight Munk made the decision, and he asked for a raise, and he was nervous, and he went over his words a thousand times in his mind.

4. It was against dad's order, and it was dangerous to take out the paddle boat during the storm, but we had to prove our manliness.

5. We finished our homework, and then we watched a horror movie on TV, and Mother treated us to two Dove bars apiece.

6. The roses bloomed. The captain promised to meet her.

7. Tyranny will be destroyed. Men feel the need for freedom.

8. Mark Gavelda was a brilliant individual, and his I. Q. could not be computed.

9. Alice phoned the bank three times. She might get the loan information for her Bolingbrook mansion.

10. Nathan Allen Sims became very ornery, and he was arrested by the policeman.

EMPHASIZING THE MAIN IDEA BY SUBORDINATING THE LESSER IDEA

In revising your first draft, you must make sure that you emphasize the important ideas by writing them in complete thoughts. Lesser ideas should be subordinated.

EXERCISE 5: In the following sentences, the main ideas have been subordinated instead of emphasized. Rewrite the ideas so that the most important idea is the main thought. Be prepared to discuss your revised sentences with the class.

Example: This loyal mood occurs on very special days such as Memorial Day, Flag Day, and the Fourth of July. This is a time **when Boy Scouts march in parades carrying the country's flag.**

In the second sentence of the example, *when Boy Scouts march in parades carrying the country's flag* is the subordinated idea. It is introduced by the subordinating conjunction *when*. Note how the writer emphasized the Boy Scouts' marching in the revised sentence.

Revised: This loyal mood occurs on very special days such as Memorial Day, Flag Day and the Fourth of July. On these special occasions, **Boy Scouts march in parades and carry the country's flag.**

1. Determined to win the tennis single's championship, **Theresa Thomas limped onto the court**. (Hint: Stress that Theresa Thomas was determined to win the tennis single's championship.)

2. Although most of the fans hope Coach Cruncher resigns as head coach, **he has given no apparent thought to the idea**. (Hint: Stress that most of the fans hope Coach Cruncher resigns as head coach.)

3. **The girls vs. boys championship volleyball game**, which was the most exciting event of the Olympiad competition, **attracted an overflow crowd into Quigley's gym**.

4. Some concert goers milled around the lobby and discussed Marvelous Melvin's performance even though the show had been over for an hour.

5. Dr. Gerrick, who is being held liable for the student's injury, left his class unattended to go to the audio-visual room.

6. Mary Beth typed 143 words per minute which prompted Dr. Procunier to hire her as the secretary for the school district.

7. A college freshman should use his time properly, and he should establish a definite study schedule, and he will received good grades at Notre Dame College.

8. Mariah listened to the Bohemian records which improved her fluency.

9. The torrential downpour flooded the 79th Street viaduct, causing drivers to detour to Columbus Boulevard.

10. Raising money for cancer research is growing more difficult because contributors have been approached by other worthwhile charities.

11. Sitting by the beach and listening to the melodious sounds of KPUX, I thought of all the advantages of being a bachelor when I realized that having a wife and raising a family are more desirable.

12. Because Lang Lee's father died and did not own an insurance policy, Lang could not afford his sophomore year of college.

13. Penny Petrulis dreamed of becoming a professional artist after her exhibit at the Beverly Arts Center received rave reviews in the local newspapers.

14. Dr. Mary Jane Nolan, the renowned author of *Mysteries of the Mind* and professor of Irish history at Lake Shore University, conducted a seminar at Waupaca High School.

15. Classes were in session at West Valley High School when the fire marshal set off the fire alarm.

To argue: to give reasons for or against something.

Argumentation is a mode of writing in which a writer uses one of her opinions as the topic of a composition. It covers an unlimited list of topics, from stockpiling nuclear weapons to eliminating the junior-senior smoking area in high school.

It differs from other expository writing in its purpose. The main purpose of the definition, analysis, process, and comparison-contrast papers is to explain. The main purpose of the argumentation paper is to convince the reader of your point of view on a specific topic. Because of its persuasive nature, argumentative writing usually adds an emotional tone which is not always present in exposition.

STAGE ONE: PREWRITING

STUDENT LEARNING OBJECTIVES

1. The student will select a controversial topic as the subject for his argumentation composition.
2. The student will state his point of view clearly and directly in the controlling idea (thesis).
3. The student will capture the reader's interest in the introductory paragraph.
4. The student will organize the details or evidence in a logical sequence.
5. The student will support his opinion with specific facts and examples.
6. The student will link the ideas using appropriate transition words and/or repeated key phrases to make the relationship of ideas clear.
7. The student will end the composition with a sense of finality.
8. The student will use specific words and sentence structures to convey a tone appropriate to the topic.

ROLE-PLAYING

In writing an **Argumentation Paper**, you must support your opinion with specific examples and organize them in a sound fashion to convince your reader of the logic of your stance.

Since you need to support your opinion with specific reasons, a good prewriting strategy is to role-play. Role-playing forces you not only to think through your position and support it with concrete examples but also to learn your opponent's point of view.

EXERCISE 1: Your class should be divided into small groups. One of the following topics can be debated with students' role-playing the different points of view.

1. Parents and students often argue over issues that "throw the house up for grabs." Select some students in your class to represent the parents' viewpoint and others to represent the students' viewpoint. Debate the following situations:
    a. High school juniors and seniors have a right to date not only on weekends but also during the week.
    b. A high school has an open policy regarding clothes, yet parents will not let their sons/daughters wear certain types of clothes to school.
    c. Parents pressure their children to receive high grades.

2. Students and administrators/teachers sometimes disagree over key school issues. Select some students to represent the students' viewpoint and others to represent the school's viewpoint and debate the following:
    a. Closed campus for all students except those involved in a work-study program.
    b. A "pit" smoking area for upperclassmen who smoke.
    c. A school dress code, specifically "outlawing" jackets, coats, and hats.
    d. Better student parking lot arrangement and facilities.
    e. Censorship by the school's administration regarding the newspaper, the school play, radio station.

3. Teachers and the school board often disagree over key issues during contract negotiations. Select some students to represent the teachers' viewpoint and other students to represent the board of education's viewpoint and debate the following:
    a. Merit pay for teachers.
    b. Three-year contract vs. one-year contract.
    c. A husband should be allowed maternity leave to take care of his wife after the birth of a child or to care for an adopted child.

WRITING PROMPTS

You must select a topic from your own experiences about which you have strong feelings and convictions and first hand knowledge. The topic must be controversial, that is, no matter how great your arguments may be, there may be some who doubt the validity of them.

The topic could also come from a writing across the curriculum assignment. In either case your primary job is to convince the reader of your side of the argument, and try to win him over to your position even though there are legitimate, opposing views.

The following topics are just suggestions to get you thinking. As a group activity you might want to discuss them and come up with alternative topics. You are free to select either side of a controversial issue--your choice.

General Topics

1. Despite protests from the National Rifle Association (NRA), hand guns should be abolished in this country.
2. All boys or all girls private high schools should be eliminated in favor of co-educational institutions.
3. A student receives a better education at a small college rather than at a large university.
4. High school enrollments should not exceed 1,000, thereby providing more opportunities for students to participate in extra-curricular activities.
5. To save on energy, homes built today should include some solar energy.
6. After narrowing down the topic, you must defend your point of view on one of these issues:
   a. Social affairs: generation gaps; racial relationships in schools; teenage involvement in community affairs.
   b. Organizations: abolishment of school extra-curricular activities because of local referendums; value of religious groups; elimination of labor unions.
   c. Politics: performance of a politician in office; current local issue such as the building of a sports stadium funded by local taxes.
   d. Health: abortion should be eliminated; cigarette smoking should not be allowed in public buildings; socialized medicine would help eliminate rising hospital costs.

7. Controversial family topics: Defend your point of view on one of these issues:

   a. Parents' discipline policy for teenagers who violate family rules, such as missing curfew, borrowing the family car.

   b. Allowances should not be given once a family member becomes a teenager.

   c. Dating age for high school students.

8. School systems should adopt the 45 days in school - -15 days out of school plan to provide year round schools instead of closing for summer vacation.

9. Advanced placement courses should be dropped because they promote intellectual elitism.

10. The Equal Rights Amendment should be passed so that women will be treated fairly and receive the same pay as men when doing the same job.

Physical Education and Driver Education

1. Students who participate in sports should not be required to take physical education class during their season. They should be given a study hall.

2. Students in drivers education should learn to drive using manual transmission instead of automatic transmission.

3. Interscholastic sports should be eliminated in favor of a school-wide intramural program.

4. There is too great an emphasis on sports in high school.

5. The National Basketball Association (NBA) should sponsor a minor league just like professional baseball does. This would eliminate many so-called student-athletes who are not academically qualified from attending college for the purpose of playing basketball.

Social Studies and Current Events

1. Defend a position on any controversial religious issue: lay apostolate; women priests; married priests; removal of churches from tax-free rules; TV evangelism.

2. Only individuals who pass an "intelligence" test at 18 years old should be eligible to vote. Otherwise, they should be required to wait until they are 21 years old.

3. Argue your point of view on a current issue, for example:

   a. Increase in foreign aid to Third World countries.

   b. U. S. policy with Japan regarding trade imbalance.

   c. Welfare system should be reviewed.

   d. Women in military service should not bear arms.

4. The United States should open up its doors to unlimited foreign immigration.

4. The United States should open up its doors to unlimited foreign immigration.

5. Take the role of either a moderate abolitionist or a radical abolitionist. After choosing your position, write an argumentative paper on how you and your colleagues are planning to solve the slavery issue. You will be trying to convince a group of Northerners that your strategy will help to abolish slavery.

6. Write an argumentative essay proving that John Marshall changed the status of the Supreme Court and that the Court, under him, strengthened the authority of the national government.

7. With your knowledge of the history of the colonies of Rhode Island and of the Carolinas, write an argumentative essay promoting the settlement by Londoners in one of the colonies and discouraging settlement in the other.

Foreign Language, Home Economics, and Shop

1. Foreign language should be taught beginning at the 3rd or 4th grade levels instead of high school.

2. Foreign languages should be eliminated from the high school curriculum because most students only memorize the vocabulary and are not capable of speaking the language once the course is finished.

3. Girls should be required to take courses in industrial arts such as electrical repair and auto repair while boys need courses in home economics such as cooking and sewing.

THINK SHEET

After you have selected your subject, jot down every bit of evidence that you think supports your opinion. You should review your facts for accuracy, realizing that some of your information might be interpreted differently, but at least knowing the rationale for your use of the evidence.

As you begin to brainstorm reasons that support your controlling idea, you should also list reasons that **oppose** your position. (Remember what you learned in your prewriting role-playing exercise.) This will not only help you understand the legitimacy of the opposite point of view but also see what arguments you might refute in the body of your paper. In fact, you might even use some of these refuted ideas in your introductory paragraph. Remember, you must respect both sides of the argument.

Name_____

Argumentation Paper Think Sheet

1. Controversial Topic____ _____

2. Intended Audience_____

3. List of specific reasons that **refute** your point of view. Provide
   concrete details.
   A. _____

   _____

   B. _____

   _____

   C. _____

   _____

4. List of specific reasons that **support** your point of view. Provide concrete
   details.
   A. _____

   _____

   B. _____

   _____

   C. _____

   _____

   D. _____

   _____

   E. _____

   _____

5. Tentative Controlling Idea_____

_____

ORGANIZING THE PAPER

Once you feel comfortable with the content on your **Think Sheet**, begin thinking in terms of the number of paragraphs to be developed. Remember, it is easier to think about a specific number of paragraphs rather than 500, 1,000, or 2,000 words. Concentrate on short term goals.

With your completed **Think Sheet** in front of you, look over your reasons, grouping similar ideas. If you have any ideas that do not support your position, subtract them from your list.

To help you organize your arguments, prioritize them from your **Think Sheet** on a piece of scratch paper, from the least important to the most important. However, instead of organizing your ideas in an order of importance sequence once you begin to write your first draft, put the second most important argument **first** and the most important argument **last**. The remaining arguments should be in the middle of the paper. Why? Your purpose is to convince your reader to agree with your point of view. Consequently, what she is going to remember most are your **first** and **last** arguments. You want to grab her attention to agree with you immediately so you hit her with a solid first punch. What she reads last is what she is going to remember most.

In each developmental paragraph you must make sure that your arguments are specific and support the controlling idea of your introductory paragraph.

COHERENCE (GLUING TOGETHER IDEAS)

Each paragraph must be linked with the preceding paragraph. Normally the order of a paper helps carry the reader from one paragraph to the next. However, in an **Argumentation Paper** the linkage of ideas is less obvious. Consequently, it is important for you to move smoothly from one thought to the next. Study the transitional words used in the model **Smokers Are Losers** on pages 144-146. Here are some transitional words to help you make the smooth transition:

Transition words for argumentation: moreover, first, second, finally, furthermore, in addition, then, too, equally important, on the contrary, hence, therefore, accordingly, thus.

INTRODUCTORY PARAGRAPHS AND AUDIENCE

Your introduction is important. You must not only include a clear statement of what you intend to prove or of what opinion you wish your audience to accept, but also you must capture their interest.

Your audience for this assignment will help determine how you begin your paper. Whom do you want to convince of your opinion?

If you are writing an argumentative essay proposing that students be allowed to date individuals of an opposite faith, for example, a Christian dating a Jewish person, your audience would be individuals who do not agree with you, possibly your parents, your girlfriend's or boyfriend's parents, or a wider audience ignorant of the situation.

If you are writing a political science essay suggesting that foreign aid is not justifiable when our own people need help, whom do you want to convince of your position?

Before you begin to write your introductory paragraph, identify your audience and think of ways of grabbing their interest. Do you want to begin with a quotation from a reliable source or an anecdote that captures the essence of your position? Do you want to begin with a series of rhetorical questions? Do you want to state your opinion firmly and use a direct statement of fact or background information introductory paragraph? The choice is yours.

You are free to use any type of introductory paragraph taught in *Fan the Deck*. However, it is probably wise to delay working on your introduction until you have established the specific arguments you will be organizing in the body of your essay.

Here are two more types of introductory paragraphs that might prove beneficial.

Startling Statement Introductory Paragraph

An interest-arousing way to begin an **Argumentation Paper** is to start with a statement that surprises the reader, excites his curiosity, and makes him want to continue reading. Observe one caution: the content of the paper should warrant this type of opening. Your purpose should not be pure sensationalism. When you use this type of introductory paragraph, the rest of the paper should explain and justify it.

Man, through his own stupidity, is destroying the earth on which he lives. He is accomplishing this by his disruption of eco-systems, which are the cycles of sustaining life. Using the guise of bettering himself, man has taken careless steps which have had disastrous effects. The elimination of an animal, the building of a structure without carefully checking out the consequences, and the destruction of a disease-carrying pest can bring all these effects forth.

Incident Introductory Paragraph

A common way to begin an **Argumentation Paper** is to present an interesting incident that is relevant to the subject and grabs the reader's interest. If you select this type of introductory paragraph, you must include a sentence which ties in the incident with the subject. Here is a student model:

Wearing a Quigley South jersey, faded blue jeans, which were cuffed at the bottom, white sweat socks and gold gym shoes, Alex walked down the main corridor of the old building. One teacher approached him saying, "That's an illegal shirt you're wearing."

"No, it's not!" Alex retorted.

"Yes, it is, and I can prove it," replied the teacher while dragging Alex into her classroom where she showed him a copy of the school dress code which plainly stated that no jerseys are to be worn in school.

Incidents like this frequently occur in high schools throughout the country, but they should not. School dress codes are ridiculous. A high school student should be judged on his academic performance, not on his style of dress.

CONCLUDING PARAGRAPHS

Your ending should be strong. If you have saved your most important argument for last, you have left your reader with the impact of a lasting impression. You might also decide to emphasize your controlling idea or proposition by restating your opinion.

As with your introductory paragraph, you can select any type of concluding paragraph already taught or the ones that follow. Whatever type you select, make sure that your ending leaves the reader with a clear understanding of your opinion.

Subject's Importance--Evaluation Concluding Paragraph

This type of concluding paragraph ends with the writer's evaluation of his argument and the consequences flowing from his evaluation. Here is a student model:

> It is man's job to keep everything running smoothly on earth. Instead, he has destroyed the balance of nature. He is kidding himself if he believes he can fix up whatever he disrupts. Man is not God. He must watch his step carefully because if he doesn't, he will cause his own extinction from the earth. The blame will be his alone, and the punishment of self-destruction will be justly deserved.

Emotional Statement or Appeal to Action Concluding Paragraph

Unless the entire tone of the paper warrants this type of ending, a writer should not use a strong emotional appeal as his final comment. This type of ending is only used when a writer wants to ask his reader to get directly involved in the subject and take some kind of action to remedy the situation. Here is a student model:

> TV viewers of America, wake up! Everyday as you comfortably sit in your cozy living room, you are being duped. You are being duped by the slick and subtle manipulators of Madison Avenue. As you focus your attention on that dramatic movie or big game, these manipulators are bombarding your subconscious with suggestions designed to line their own pockets--that super VCR, that ranch mink stole, that exotic South Sea island trip. Until you realize what's going on, you will be the loser, the only loser.

STAGE TWO: WRITING THE FIRST DRAFT

With your completed **Think Sheet** in front of you, write your first draft. Do not be concerned with errors. Just get your content on paper.

As you write, think of your audience. Keep their opinions in mind. Be open-minded. Convince them of your opinion by being honest and straightforward. You have collected the data, and now you are presenting the information in a logical sequence.

If you are refuting arguments against your position, be considerate and tactful. Your purpose is to win them over, not turn them against you.

TONE IN ARGUMENTATION

You have one final point to consider as you write your first draft--tone. Tone is a writer's attitude toward his subject and audience. A reader can determine a writer's tone by examining the sentence structures and word choices, especially the word choices.

Each word that a writer uses has a denotative and a connotative meaning. The denotative meaning is the exact meaning of a word. For example, the exact meaning of the word *father* is male parent. Rather cold and formal, isn't it?

The connotative meaning of a word is the implied meaning, the emotional feeling a word provides. *Father* suggests love, warmth, making chicken paprikas, worrying after a baseball loss, joking about zippers on pockets, suffering, caring, always caring.

In writing an argumentative essay, you must be careful of the words that you select. Since your main purpose is to convince your audience of your opinion, it is advisable that you use words that project a positive impression. For example, if you were trying to convince someone to buy a Macintosh computer, you might use words like *user friendly, simple, not complicated commands, enthusiasm of Mac owners, easy, computer will not let you make a mistake,* etc. Select your words carefully.

Now write your first draft.

STAGE THREE: REWRITING

SENTENCE OPENING SHEET

By now you should be accustomed to using the **Sentence Opening Sheet** as a practical guide in helping you revise your first draft. If you need to review the specific purposes for each of the four columns, refer to pages 18-20 from the **definition paper**.

For this assignment we want you to concentrate on column number two, the special word column. In your other major writing assignments in *Fan*, you have probably listed *teacher pet peeve words* or *dead words*, words your teacher wanted you to avoid on your final draft.

Now we want you to list the *tone* words you included in your first draft. If you cannot list any *tone* words in column two, maybe you need to expand. Since *tone* words make an emotional appeal that help persuade your audience to agree with your opinion, you should use them on your final draft.

PEER EVALUATION USING A CHECKLIST SHEET

In critiquing your partner's composition, make sure she follows the objectives as stated on the **Students Objectives and Evaluation Sheet** your teacher distributed during the prewriting stage.

EXERCISE 1: Before you exchange papers with your proofreading partner or begin your exchange in your support group, read and discuss the following student model. Use the guide questions from the **Checklist Sheet**.

Smokers Are Losers

(A)   WARNING: THE SURGEON GENERAL HAS DETERMINED THAT CIGARETTE SMOKING MAY BE HAZARDOUS TO YOUR HEALTH. Despite this warning found on every cigarette pack and on every cigarette advertisement in the nation, millions of people ignore this warning. For Americans, cigarettes are more deadly than bullets, germs, and viruses. Unfortunately, most people still feel that the risks associated with smoking always take their toll on "someone else." The deadly poisons in cigarette smoke have their greatest effect on the most vital and life sustaining systems of the body--the respiratory and circulatory systems.

(B)   Of all the body processes that are harmed by cigarette smoke, the one that is publicized the most and receives the greatest injury is the respiratory system. Smokers are seventy times more likely to have lung cancer than non-smokers. The tar in cigarette smoke mixes with mucus and bacteria and collects in the lungs to form festering pools, resulting in lung tissue degeneration and reducing the amount of oxygen transferred to the blood.

(C)   Carbon monoxide, the deadly gas found in automobile exhausts, is present in large amounts in cigarette smoke, along with other substances such as hydrogen, cyanide, formaldehyde, and nicotine. Any of these substances could kill a man, were it not for the body's filtering systems.

(D)   Many smokers think that these systems can "take care of it all," but the truth is that these systems become overloaded and soon have little effect on the poisons in cigarette smoke. The "tar" in cigarettes, when collected and applied to skin of mice in the laboratory, produces cancer within a few days. Smoking is also known to cause emphysema and bronchitis, as well as lowering the body's resistance to disease.

(E)   Despite smoking's effect on the lungs, its damage to the heart can be more severe. Scientific studies have shown that carbon monoxide in cigarette smoke, present at 400 times the level considered safe in industry, greatly reduces the oxygen content of the blood. At the same time, the nicotine in the smoke causes the smoker's heart rate, heart output, and blood pressure to rise. Thus, the heart needs more oxygen just when the body's oxygen supply is at its lowest.

(F)   Nicotine puts a tremendous strain on the heart muscle by causing small blood vessels to contract, further restricting blood flow. If the smoker's body were to absorb all the nicotine in just one puff of cigarette smoke, he would die within a few minutes, but since some of the nicotine is destroyed by the cigarette's heat, its only result is a slow, steady, killing strain on the heart muscle.

(G)   Besides increasing the heart rate, nicotine, along with the other poisons in cigarette smoke, raises the level of cholesterol in the bloodstream, increasing the formation of fatty deposits on the walls of veins and arteries, which results in coronary heart disease and arteriosclerosis (hardening of the arteries). Cigarette smoke also causes blood platelets to stick together, forming blood clots which can lead to crippling or fatal strokes.

(H)   Cigarette smoke also has many other adverse effects upon the body and its functions. Smoking lessens physical endurance and deadens the senses of taste and smell, as well as reducing the appetite. Because of this loss of appetite associated with smoking, many smokers claim they smoke to lose weight. Nonsense! What use is a slim corpse? Lung cancer and heart disease are a great price to pay for the small amount of weight loss involved.

(I)   Cancer of the lip, mouth, and tongue are widespread among smokers, not to mention the increased rate of cancer in all parts of the body, since at least 30 of the compounds in cigarette smoke have been found to cause cancer in laboratory animals. Deaths from ulcers of the stomach and intestines are four times as frequent in smokers than in non-smokers.

(J)   Smoking also can effect vision, and along with alcohol, contributes to the onset of cirrhosis of the liver. Cigarette smoke depresses the reflexes and causes accidents, not to mention the many fatal fires started each year by smokers. An automobile's exhaust is actually less poisonous than cigarette smoke! Other bad effects of smoking are loss of teeth, stained teeth, and bad breath. Non-smokers who inhale cigarette smoke are affected the same ways as smokers, although to a much lesser degree.

(K)   All of these statistics prove that smokers, through their persistent habit, are leading themselves to an early grave. We all know smokers we love personally. Their lives can be saved by others who heed the warnings issued by doctors, scientists, and other researchers and who are determined enough to force the smoker to give up his attitude of indifference for one of concern for himself. There has been much talk about developing a completely safe cigarette, but in reality, the only safe cigarette is the one that is kept at a safe distance.

Writer's Name_____

Evaluator's Name_____

Argumentation Paper Checklist

Introductory Paragraph

1. What is the writer's opinion as stated in the controlling idea?

2. How does the introductory paragraph capture your interest?

Developmental Paragraphs

3. What is the overall organization of the body of the composition? In other words, did the writer use some type of order of importance sequence or did he just enumerate his arguments?

4. How does each idea support the writer's purpose?

5. Has the writer effectively used transitional words or repeated key ideas to make the transition smooth between paragraphs?

Concluding Paragraph

6. Does the concluding paragraph effectively end the composition by presenting either the last argument or restating the opinion from the controlling idea?

Tone

7. What tone words did the writer include in the composition to help you be convinced of his opinion?

Style and Mechanics

8. Edit your partner's paper checking for fragments, run-ons, verb tense consistency, variety in sentence openings and structures, faulty parallelism, etc. **Be a friend.**

9. Tell your partner the **best** thing you like about his argumentative essay.

STAGE FOUR: PUBLISHING

Before you turn in your final draft, find someone who disagrees with your point of view on your controversial topic and read your composition to him. Ask him the following questions. After listening to my composition, do you at least understand my position on this issue? Have I persuaded you to agree with my position? Do you at least have a better understanding of the other side?

Argumentative essays also are excellent topics for speeches.

Finally, you might want to include this essay in your writing portfolio.

All the writing assignments in *Fan the Deck* have been selected to prepare you for similar assignments in college. Probably the most difficult writing assignment you will experience in college is writing a research report, which is usually longer and more complex than your normal assignments. Consequently, we end *Fan the Deck* with this type of paper so that you will be confident when six of your professors assign research reports due the first day after the Christmas holidays.

In this **Problem-Solution Report Unit**, you will be required to write about a newsworthy current problem, explain the extent of the problem and its effects on people, examine its causes, and present a viable solution(s). In order to do this properly, you will be asked to do research in your school or public library. Therefore, with this paper, you will learn the techniques of research report writing and practice these techniques before you write the final draft.

Be alert and keep up with daily assignments which will present a step-by-step process to develop a problem-solution report. We have *stacked the deck* so that your hard work will lead to a satisfying experience and a satisfactory paper. All you have to do is to follow these steps:

Step　1:　Choose a newsworthy current problem.
Step　2:　Write a tentative controlling idea--thesis statement.
Step　3:　Compile a working bibliography on all sources (books, magazine articles, and reference works) that have information on your topic.
Step　4:　Take notes on information that tell about the extent, effects, causes, and solutions to the problem.
Step　5:　Use your notes to complete a **Think Sheet** which will serve as your outline.
Step　6:　Write the first draft of short term goals, that is, the body of your report.
Step　7:　Write the introduction.
Step　8:　Write the conclusion.
Step　9:　Complete a **Sentence Opening Sheet** to help you analyze your writing.
Step 10:　Exchange your first draft for peer evaluation.
Step 11:　Revise your first draft.
Step 12:　Write the footnote or endnote page.
Step 13:　Write the bibliography page.
Step 14:　Write the final draft.

STAGE ONE: PREWRITING

STUDENT LEARNING OBJECTIVES

1. The student will write a problem-solution report about a current problem.
2. The student will divide the report into six short term goals: introduction, extent of the problem, effects of the problem, causes of the problem, solution(s) of the problem, and conclusion.
3. The student will state her main idea in the controlling idea or thesis.
4. The student will supply specific information about the problem-solution.
5. The student will take notes and use the information in the paper's footnotes.
6. The student will write a bibliography, listing the sources of information.

WRITING PROMPT AND PURPOSE

Your assignment is to write a research report in which you identify a problem, research it, and based upon your research, come up with a viable solution(s) to the problem. You have two **purposes**. First, in a well-organized report you want **to inform** your audience of what the problem is. Specifically, you want them to know the extent of the problem, its effects on the population, and its causes. Second, you want **to present** a specific solution(s) to the problem.

Since this is a research report, you will be expected to compile a bibliography of sources, take notes, and footnote where necessary. The choice of which problem you select is **yours**. However, since you will be spending a considerable amount of time working on this report, consider the following suggestions.

1. Select a problem that **interests you**. As long as you are going to spend many hours working on this report, you might as well study something that you are already interested in or would enjoy investigating. If you select a problem that is boring for you, you will not spend the necessary time to find out more about it.

2. Select a subject on which **materials are available** in your school library or nearby college and public libraries. You might have to make a preliminary check to see if the materials are available. Since you are expected to compile a bibliography and take notes, it would be foolish to select a topic and then not be able to investigate it thoroughly.

STUDENT MODEL

Before you begin the step-by-step process of writing a problem-solution report, read and discuss the following student report written by a high school senior from Portland, Oregon, who followed the problem-solution process outlined in this unit. We have listed her short term goals in the left margin.

SUICIDE: A TEENAGE EPIDEMIC

Introduction

Attractive, intelligent, and always considerate of people around her, Amy was the kind of girl every parent would like to raise. But Amy did not like herself, so she decided to change her image. Soon she started shoplifting, letting her grades drop, and acting rude and unfriendly. Two weeks after her personality change, Amy was found dead in her bedroom holding an empty bottle of sleeping pills.

Like Amy, David was a good person, except lately he had seemed obsessed with death. So, whenever he mentioned suicide, everyone just shrugged it off and told him to quit talking so "silly." That same week, David hanged himself in the garage.[1] In both cases, the suicides might have been prevented if someone had noticed the signals sent out by Amy and David. **Since suicide**
Thesis
is cry for help, it must be answered by those around to hear it.

Extent of the Problem

Suicide among young people has almost become an epidemic. Suicide has risen from the 5th cause of death in 1972 to the 3rd leading cause of death among teenagers in 1982. Around 60% of the suicide deaths are boys, but girls make up 90% of the total suicide attempts.[2] Even though suicide attempts outnumber the actual deaths 50 to 1, thousands of young people die as a result of suicide each year.[3] Approximately 30% of these teenagers are dropouts; moreover, around 70% come from broken or disrupted homes.[4]

Effects of the Problem

These disrupted homes are even further troubled by the death of these young suicides. Suicides affect the entire family. The surviving family members feel a lot of hurt, anger, fright, even guilt. The parents of a suicide victim seem to feel guilt and responsibility towards the incident. Usually, the parents want to know where they went wrong with their child. However, it is the siblings of the suicide victim who are left the most confused, with questions as to why the disaster occurred. On top of the confusion, the children are filled with disbelief and shock.

151

Although the family finally accepts the suicide, a whole new feeling sets in. Many times the family feels resentment towards the suicide, and as a result, usually the parents blame themselves. Nobody denies the fact that everyone suffers when someone close to them dies, but suicide, an unexpected, sometimes brutal death, leaves lasting scars of hurt and resentment on the family. What many families would like to forget is the way the young suicide died. Although girls who commit suicide are usually more passive, using sleeping pills or slitting their wrists, they are quickly becoming more violent. Like the boys, the girls are beginning to hang themselves and use guns to end their lives.[5]

Causes of the Problem

Aside from the way teenagers are dying, people want to know why the self-inflicted deaths are happening. While no one knows of any set reason, it is known that suicides start from confusion, disappointment, and/or depression.[6] In fact, "the conflicting values of what the adolescent believes and what he sees in the world around him create turmoil, hostility, and disappointment."[7] Some teenagers think that problems should solve themselves. But when this does not happen they do not know how to handle their problems, and the teenagers become frustrated, even self-destructive.

Teenagers feel a lack of communication between themselves and others that could help them work out their problems. This lack of communication and tension at home, caused by divorce, frequent moving, or severe money problems, can make a young person feel unsure or insecure about his surroundings. When a teenager must deal with feelings of insecurity at home and confusion of life, he sometimes finds that the only solution is suicide.

Overprotectiveness is another factor in many suicides.[8] The young adult feels as if he is being "babied" by his parents, and as a result, rebels by trying things on his own. Many times, though, the person fails, resulting in humiliation and loss of self-confidence, even thoughts of suicide. But what about the kids who seem to come from good surroundings who commit suicide? These suicides are the ones caused by lack of self-love. For example, a teenager is having a hard time liking himself despite the fact that most everyone else does. After a long period of time, this self-hatred builds, making all problems bigger than they really are. After awhile, life is too much to handle, and another teen commits suicide.

Solutions to the Problem

Surely the number of deaths can be reduced if people respond to the potential victim's cries for help. More often than not, suicidal people send out signals which need to be picked up. One of the main signals is personality change. For example, an honor student stops studying, a quiet person suddenly becomes loud and obnoxious, and an easy-going person becomes shy and withdrawn.[9]

Along with these changes that may be hard to detect, there are more obvious signals. Actions such as someone giving away his most prized possession, the attitude of not caring anymore, and a complete obsession with death are signals that should never be ignored.

If someone suspects a friend of contemplating suicide, he should confront the person. Questions directed towards the suicidal person should be asked calmly, yet sincerely so the person sees real concern.[10] Communication is the key solution. In other words, "if we want to stop the suicide epidemic, we must break the conspiracy that surrounds it."[11]

Some Colorado high schools are working on opening up those communication lines. High schoolers in these schools take a required class in suicide prevention that not only teaches them to cope and understand suicide but also teaches four very important things teenagers need to know for themselves. First of all, self-esteem is taught. Teenagers need to know that their value lies in who they are, not in what they do. Secondly, communication skills are taught so that high schoolers can learn to express themselves and discuss how they feel. Along with self-esteem and communication skills, these kids are taught about posi-failure, accepting the effort a person puts out as positive, no matter what the outcome is. The fourth thing taught in this class is how to handle grief. Many suicides result from a feeling of loss because teenagers do not know how to handle losing a close relative or friend, a cherished pet, or something meaningful to them.[12] With the help of everyone involved with teenagers, many suicides could be avoided.

Conclusion   The problem of suicide can only be solved if the people around act on the desperate cry for help. If you were on the edge of committing suicide, wouldn't you want someone to talk to, someone to care? I challenge you, the reader, to watch for signals or at least to be aware of them. Also, try to build up people, especially young people in your life, by giving them a little more self-confidence.

In today's busy world, a lot of teenagers are pushed around and left confused with no one to turn to. But when the hurt and depression lead to death, confusion becomes real, affecting whole family. Just remember, young people have many little problems that need solving. With a little help and direction, these problems can be stopped from becoming too big for a teenager to handle. After all, some kids think suicide is the only way out. But really, "suicide is a permanent solution to a temporary problem."[13]

SUGGESTED TOPICS

In case you have not already thought of a problem you wish to report on, here are some possibilities. Discuss how the question can be stated as a specific problem.

1. Who should decide which books are suitable for a library? (Censorship)
2. Should surrogate motherhood be encouraged as an alternative means to parenthood?
3. Have sports become too violent? (You might want to narrow this to a sport such as football, hockey or the like.)
4. How can racism be eliminated in our society?
5. Which, if any, illegal aliens should be granted citizen status?
6. Will capital punishment ultimately reduce crime?
7. Should creationism be taught in public schools?
8. Do electronic games exert a negative influence on children?
9. How severe a crime is cheating or cribbing in school?
10. Should our government bail out major corporations in financial trouble, e.g., Chrysler Motors?
11. What can be done about teen runaways?
12. Who are the poor in America and what can be done to help them?
13. Is "not guilty by reason of insanity" a legitimate defense?
14. How can the costs of medical care be cut?
15. Is our penal system too severe? too lenient?
16. How ethical are college athletic recruiting practices?
17. Whose responsibility are the elderly, and what kind of services do they have a right to expect?
18. Should teachers be allowed to strike?
19. Should prisons be rehabilitative or punitive?
20. Are computerized businesses invading our privacy?
21. Should euthanasia be a personal decision?
22. Is genetic engineering an ethical or legal issue?
23. How should the legal system handle the kidnapping of a child by one of his own parents?
24. Are computers and/or robots replacing people in industry?
25. Should there be exceptions to the minimum wage law?
26. Will stronger hand gun control help curb the rise in violent crime?
27. How far can the CIA or FBI go in dealing with national security issues?
28. What can be done about obesity in America?
29. What can be done to curb U. S. drug use?
30. Is there too much sex/violence on television? in movies?
31. Is space exploration worth the money?
32. Should animals be used for medical or scientific experimentation?
33. What can be done about parents who abuse their children?
34. Are convalescent homes adequately treating our elderly?
35. Should public funds be used to provide special services for the handicapped?

154

EXERCISE 1: Select three of the above questions as possible topics for your problem-solution report. Rewrite the questions as specific problems.

EXERCISE 2: As a group activity, brainstorm other possible problems that affect you directly and that can serve as topics for this final writing assignment, especially writing across the curriculum problems.

Special Hint: If you have difficulty selecting a topic for this problem-solution report, think about the different segments you have seen on *60 Minutes* or *Dateline*. These programs are always dealing with current newsworthy problems.

CONTROLLING IDEA (THESIS STATEMENT)

With your problem selected, you should write a controlling idea (thesis statement) just as you have done for the other writing assignments in *Fan the Deck*. A problem-solution report needs a main idea to give focus to your research. The thesis statement of this paper should state the problem and the solution.

Combine I (the statement of the problem) and II (the statement of the solution) into a complex sentence (using subordinating conjunctions) or into a compound sentence (with coordinating conjunctions--**BOYS FAN**).

Complex Sentence

A. _____   _____,
    (Subordinator)   (Problem)

_____.
(Solution)

Example 1:

    Problem: Home burglaries are increasing rapidly.
    Solution: Homeowners must not only become aware of the problem but also take preventive measures to eliminate home burglaries.

    Thesis: **If (SUBORDINATOR)** the ever increasing home burglary rate is to be cut **(PROBLEM)**, homeowners must become aware of the problem and take measures to prevent intrusion into their homes **(SOLUTION)**.

Example 2:

> **Problem:** The whale is an endangered species.
> **Solution:** Whale products should be taken off the market.
>
> **Thesis:** **Since (Subordinator)** <u>the whale is an endangered species</u>
> **(PROBLEM)**, <u>all whale products should be taken off the market.</u>
> **(SOLUTION)**.

Compound Sentence

B. _____, _____
   (Problem)   (Coordinator)

   _____ .
   (Solution)

Example 1:

> **Problem:** Many elementary students do not have the basic skills when entering
> high school.
> **Solution:** Early childhood education centers will help youngsters acquire the
> necessary skills to prepare them for high school.
>
> **Thesis:** <u>Elementary school graduates need basic skills before entering high</u>
> <u>school</u> **(PROBLEM)**, **and (COORDINATOR)** <u>sufficient federal</u>
> <u>funding for early education centers will help prepare students with</u>
> <u>the right skills.</u> **(SOLUTION)**.

Example 2:

> **Problem:** Health standards are deteriorating in nursing homes.
> **Solution:** Visitations by officials and family members and friends will help
> improve the standards of nursing homes.
>
> **Thesis:** <u>Health standards in US. nursing homes are decreasing rapidly</u>
> **(PROBLEM)**, **so (COORDINATOR)** <u>they must be checked by</u>
> <u>frequent visits by state and federal officials as well as by friends and</u>
> <u>family of the patients.</u> **(SOLUTION)**.

EXERCISE 3: On a piece of scratch paper, write your tentative controlling idea (thesis statement) for your problem topic. You might practice with some of the problems from the suggested list on page 154. Some of your thesis statements might be duplicated for class discussion. Save your final thesis for your introductory paragraph.

1. State the problem you are writing about here. Write a complete sentence. (e.g. *Students have too much homework.)*

_____

_____

_____

2. State a general solution here. Write a complete sentence. (e.g. *They should have more class time to complete it.)*

_____

_____

_____

3. Now, combine sentence 1 with sentence 2 to make a tentative controlling idea (thesis). (*Because students have too much homework, they should be allowed more class time to complete it.)*

_____

_____

_____

PREPARING A WORKING BIBLIOGRAPHY

Now that you have selected a problem and written a tentative controlling idea, you need to compile a working bibliography of books, magazine articles, pamphlets, etc., sources of information for your problem-solution report. If you have acccss to the **internet**, try searching the World Wide Web or some other on-line resources. If you use specific information (even if you put it in your own words) or the exact words from an article in a magazine, book, or a reference work, you must give credit to your source. Therefore, you should keep a record of all the sources you might use to get information for your report.

Write your working bibliography on either 3 x 5 or 4 x 6 inch index cards. You should write only one reference per card and include the following information:

--Author's name, last name first.
--Title of article, book, encyclopedia, and/or periodical.
--Place of publication.
--Publisher.
--Date of publication.
--Volume number (if applicable).
--Page numbers (if applicable).

Once you have collected your working bibliography, arrange your cards in alphabetical order by author or title. Use a rubber band to keep your cards together. You might want to keep your cards in a small index box.

Study the two bibliography cards prepared by Leanne Michener, the writer of the **Suicide: A Teenage Epidemic** report on pages 151-153.

Bibliography Card - Book

Author's Name	Klagburn, Francine
Title of Book	Youth and Suicide, Too Young to Die
Place of Publication	New York
Publisher	Pocket Books
Year	1976

Bibliography Card - Magazine

Author's Name	Felsenthal, Carol Greenberg
Title of Article	"Teen Suicide"
Magazine	Seventeen
Volume and Pages	Volume 38, Page 184
Date of Issue	April, 1979

EXERCISE 4: Find a least five sources of information for your problem-solution report. Prepare a bibliography card for each source.

MAKING A PRELIMINARY OUTLINE

With your problem already chosen and a tentative controlling idea written, you are ready to prepare a preliminary outline to serve as your guide in your reading and note-taking. This is one of the most difficult parts of writing a research report. Now you need to think about your topic and the questions you want to answer in your report. You need to plan on the short term goals you want to accomplish in your assignment.

For this final assignment in *Fan the Deck*, we are going to make it easier by presenting some specific short term goals you might decide to use in organizing your report, just as the writer did in the **Suicide: A Teenage Epidemic** model.

Your problem-solution report could consist of six short term goals:

Goal 1--Introduction

You must write an introduction similar to those you have written so far in *Fan the Deck*. Later in this unit we will provide seven possible methods you may use to begin your report. End your introduction with a thesis statement which lets your audience know what will be proven in your paper.

Goal 2--Extent of the Problem

Here you will need to explain the scope and magnitude of your problem.

Goal 3--Effects of the Problem

In this section you will need to answer some basic questions. What are the effects of the problem? What is the problem doing to the people affected?

Goal 4--Causes of the Problem

Why does the problem exist? Your causes may include physical, social, economic, emotional, other factors, or a combination of the above.

Goal 5--Solutions to the Problem

Make clear the procedure and methods needed to solve the problem. Some problems may call for more than one solution. Keep in mind such factors as cost, time, and manpower. You might show where some similar solutions have worked at another time or another place.

Goal 6--Conclusion

Your conclusion has two purposes: to restate the thesis (in different words) and to bring your paper to an end. Later we will present three methods for concluding this problem-solution report.

TAKING NOTES

Now that your working bibliography is completed and you have a preliminary outline (remember the short term goals above), you should begin to read and takes notes on your topic.

As you begin to read the sources from your working bibliography, think about the four major goals in the body of your paper: extent, effects, causes, and solutions to the problem. Whenever you find information related to one of your goals, prepare a specific note card.

Take as many notes as you can in your own words, keeping to the same ideas as the original book, article, or entry. You need not write in complete sentences. Just make sure you understand what you have written down so that you do not have to go back again to the original source.

Here are some more guidelines for you in note-taking:

- Use either 3 x 5 or 4 x 6 inch index cards.
- Each item of information should be recorded on its own index card.
- Write notes in your own words.
- If you feel that you want to quote directly, write down the exact words and enclose the words in quotation marks.
- Make sure you identify the source of the information in the upper right hand corner.
- Mark the page number on the bottom of the card.
- On the top of the card you should include the division from your preliminary outline: extent, effects, causes, and solutions.

Here is a sample note from the **Suicide: A Teenage Epidemic** report:

Extent of the Problem   *Miller*

Teenagers from broken homes =
70% of suicide victims

                                                    page 68

EXERCISE 5: Before you begin to take notes on your problem-solution report, write out a bibliography card and practice taking notes from the following Congressional *Quarterly's Editorial Research Reports* pamphlet entitled *Troubled Teenagers,* Volume 2, Number 2, July 17, 1987, pages 346-360.

If you were writing a paper on teenage suicide, you could use the information from this source. Read the paragraphs on the top of the next page, taking notes after you read them. Be sure you identify your source, label your subtopic (extent, effects, causes, solutions), and give the page number(s). Compare your notes with your classmates. These paragraphs appeared on page 152.

The most extreme way of not dealing with life is, of course, suicide. Each year, more than 5,000 youths--about one-third of them teenagers and most of the rest in their early 20's--kill themselves. Most (three-fourths) are white males. Many more youths attempt suicide and still more think seriously about it. Since 1960, the suicide rate for youths 15-24 has more than doubled--to 12.5 per 100,000 in 1984, about the same as the rate for the general population.

What accounts for this disturbing trend? Charlotte P. Ross, president and executive director of the Youth Suicide National Center in Washington, D. C., says that-- on top of the usual pressures and pains of adolescence--many more teenagers today than in the past have "pretty important losses" earlier in their lives, thanks to divorces or family moves, and many more teenagers today also have a "severely weakened or damaged support system. You put the package together and you've got a very fertile field for suicidal behavior."

Most teenagers, wanting their parents to see them as succeeding and maturing, Ross says, will not tell them about their hurts or perceived failures. They need adults who know them well enough and see them often enough to be able to perceive their troubles without being told and then to give them support and guidance. "We have a lot of kids today," she says, " who, in essence, sort of grow up in isolation."

Now begin your research.

THINK SHEET

Now that you have taken all your notes, you are ready to organize them in a sequence that will demonstrate orderly thinking. Group your note cards into the main divisions of your paper: extent, effects, causes, and solution(s), if you have followed our suggestions. If you have used some additional divisions, organize your note cards accordingly.

In looking over your note cards, you might have to rename some of them and discard others as you categorize your ideas.

The purpose of this **Think Sheet** is to organize your notes by specific goals. The **Think Sheet** has each short term goal outlined with a column for the note and a column for the source and page number. If you find that you have very little to put under any of the four short term goal entries, you may wish to go to the library for more information. Complete this **Think Sheet** on your own paper. This serves as your outline. Also, make sure that each short term goal has its own controlling idea which supports the report's overall purpose.

Name_____

Problem-Solution   Report Think Sheet

1. Write your thesis statement._____

_____

2. In what way is your topic controversial? _____

_____

In Column #1, list the specific supports (facts, statistics, quotes) from note cards.

In Column #2, write the source and page number.

COLUMN I	**COLUMN II**

1. **EXTENT** (What is the scope and magnitude of the problem?)

A. _____ | _____

B. _____ | _____

C. _____ | _____

D. _____ | _____

E. _____ | _____

F. _____ | _____

G. _____ | _____

CONTROLLING IDEA--extent of problem_____

_____

2. EFFECTS (What happened because of the problem?)

A. _____

B. _____

C. _____

D. _____

E. _____

F. _____

G. _____

CONTROLLING IDEA--effects of the problem_____

_____

3. CAUSES (Why does the problem exist?)

A. _____

B. _____

C. _____

D. _____

E. _____

F. _____

G. _____

CONTROLLING IDEA--causes of the problem_____

_____

4. SOLUTION(S) (What can be done to eliminate or reduce the problem?)

A. _____ | _____

B. _____ | _____

C. _____ | _____

D. _____ | _____

E. _____ | _____

F. _____ | _____

G. _____ | _____

CONTROLLING IDEA--solution(s) of the problem_____

_____

STAGE TWO: WRITING THE FIRST DRAFT

Before you begin to write your first draft, read your notes two or three times to know them fully. This helps you focus on the ideas you want to stress instead of simply copying from your note cards and/or **Think Sheet**.

Now, using the **Think Sheet** and/or your note cards as your guide, write your first draft of the problem-solution report, skipping every other line. Each of the sections of your **Think Sheet** should be a short term goal in the body of your report. Each will need to be expanded with your own words. Do not simply string together a series of quotes. Use transition words.

Feel free to change the order of importance within each section to fit your needs. Be sure that you concentrate on organization and that your ideas follow logically. Use specific details and quotations from your notes. Give credit to sources where you have made use of them in your paper. Write the source and page number in the margin opposite a direct quote or fact that you want to include.

INTRODUCTORY PARAGRAPH

Since you have been concentrating on the content of your report, it should be easy for you to write your introduction after you have worked on the body of the report just as you have done with other assignments in *Fan the Deck*. Here are some possible methods of developing your introduction.

A. A Specific Example. Present a specific instance of the problem.

B. Rhetorical Questions. Ask the audience a series of questions which will arouse interest.

C. A Shocking Statement. Make an opening statement which startles the audience and which at the same time leads directly to the problem.

D. A Quotation. Use a saying. Often short quotations contain the essence of the whole problem.

E. A Series of Examples. Begin by presenting in rapid-fire fashion a series of instances of the problem. Overwhelm the audience with the enormity of the problem.

F. Misunderstanding. Suggest a common mistake or misunderstanding that the report intends to correct.

G. Then-Now Contrast. Show the problem as it once was and how it is now. Emphasize how the problem is getting worse.

Page 102 lists the different types of introductory paragraphs included in *Fan*.

Remember, your introduction should capture your audience's interest and let them know the purpose of your paper. It should contain your thesis, which you practiced writing earlier in this unit, page 155.

CONCLUDING PARAGRAPH

Since you have studied many different types of concluding paragraphs, the choice of which type to use is yours. However, your ending should have several sentences and give a sense of finality to the paper. You might also include a restated thesis in your conclusion, either as the first or last sentence, whichever sounds best. Your restated thesis should use different words.

Page 102 lists different types of concluding paragraphs. Here are three other possible ways of ending your report:

A. Challenge your audience to do something. Tell the reader what he can do to help solve the problem.

B. Use a key quotation. Sometimes a quotation sums up the main point or prevailing feeling of the paper.

C. Show how your subject fits into a larger picture. Show how your topic (problem) is part of or leads to a bigger problem.

Now write your first draft.

STAGE THREE: REWRITING

SENTENCE OPENING SHEET

After you have written your first draft report, complete the **Sentence Opening Sheet** as directed by your teacher. By now you should be aware of the specific types of mistakes the **SOS** sheet helps you to identify. Here is one final review:

- Variety in sentence openings and sentence lengths.
- Elimination of teacher pet peeve or dead words.
- Strong, active verbs.
- Use of active instead of passive voice.
- Consistent verb tenses.
- Consistent point of view.
- Elimination of fragments and run-ons.
- Short sentences to emphasize key ideas.
- Subtraction of unnecessary words and ideas.

PEER EVALUATION USING A CHECKLIST SHEET

Just as you have with the other assignments in *Fan*, you will be exchanging reports with a partner or in a small support group. Follow the same procedure as you have up to now.

Concentrate on the stated objectives as listed on the **Student Objectives and Evaluation Sheet** distributed by your teacher. Since this project is much more demanding and complex than your other assignments, you might need to spend more time evaluating your partner's paper. Do not rush through the evaluation. Anything worth doing is worth doing well.

Writer's Name_____

Evaluator's Name_____

Problem-Solution Report Checklist

Introductory Paragraph

1. Which of the seven introductory paragraphs did the writer use? Is the problem clearly stated?

Developmental Paragraphs

2. Is there clearly one division that deals with the *extent* of the problem? the *effects* of the problem? the *causes* of the problem? Is there a clear *solution* or *solutions*?

3. Check for generalizations. Does your writer's report clearly give evidence and support the statements made?

4. Has credit been given for each direct quote? Has credit been given to other information (facts, statistics, ideas) that come from a researched source?

Concluding Paragraph

5. Which of the three types of conclusions did the writer use? How was it effective?

Endnotes and Bibliography

6. Did the writer follow the proper format for the endnotes and bibliography as instructed by your teacher?

FINAL COPY AFTER PEER EVALUATION--TITLE PAGE, ENDNOTES, BIBLIOGRAPHY

With this report you need a title page. The title of the paper and your name should be in the middle of the page. Your class, teacher's name, and date should be listed in the lower right corner of the page.

Since you have used footnotes in your paper, you will need to include a footnote page, or endnote page, that lists the source for each footnote. List them in consecutive numerical order on a separate sheet instead of on the bottom of the page in the completed manuscript.

Because you used several sources to find information for your problem-solution report, you will need to list them in alphabetical order on a separate piece of paper. If you wrote down the necessary information as you wrote your bibliography cards, the bibliography is almost finished.

Here are samples of a title page, endnote page, and bibliography from the **Suicide: A Teenage Epidemic** report.

Suicide: A Teenage Epidemic

by

Leanne Michener

Advanced Composition
Mr. Hanna
September 9, 2003

SAMPLE ENDNOTES OR FOOTNOTES

Endnotes

[1]Carol Greenberg Felsenthal, "Teen Suicide," *Seventeen*, 38 (April, 1979), p. 184.

[2]Mary Susan Miller, "Teen Suicide," *Ladies Home Journal*, 94 (February, 1977), p. 68.

[3]James P. Comer, "Young Suicides," *Parents*, 57 (August, 1982), p. 88.

[4]Miller, p. 68.

[5]Francine Klagsbrun, *Youth and Suicide, Too Young to Die* (New York, Pocket Books, 1976), pp. 100-102.

[6]Margaret O. Hyde and Elizabeth Held, M. D., *Suicide, the Hidden Epidemic* (New York, Franklin Watts, 1978), p. 16.

[7]Miller, p. 72.

[8]Miller, pp. 72-74.

[9]Felsenthal, p.185.

[10]Comer, p. 88.

[11]Mary Ann O'Roark, "The Alarming Rise in Teenage Suicide," *macaws*, 109, (January, 1982), p.12.

[12]O'Roark, p. 12.

[13]O'Roark, p. 14.

We have provided a general format to follow in footnoting. Your school might use the *MLA Style Sheet* or some other research handbook. Your teacher will probably provide you with special instructions for footnoting in order that you follow your school's policy.

Here are some simple guidelines to follow in preparing your final bibliography:

1. Arrange all entries in alphabetical order, by the last name of the author or editor first.
2. Single space with each entry but double space between sources.
3. Indent the run-on lines of each source.
4. Do not number your sources.
5. Follow the format given to you by your teacher.

SAMPLE BIBLIOGRAPHY

BIBLIOGRAPHY

Comer, James P., "Young Suicides," *Parents*, 57, August, 1982, p. 88.

Felsenthal, Carol Greenberg, "Teen Suicide," *Seventeen*, 38, April, 1979, pp. 184+.

Hyde, Margaret O., and Elizabeth Forsyth, M. D., *Suicide, the Hidden Epidemic,* New York, Franklin Watts, 1978.

Klagsbrun, Francine, *Youth and Suicide, Too Young to Die,* New York, Pocket Books, 1976.

Miller, Mary Susan, "Teen Suicide," *Ladies Home Journal*, 94, February, 1977, pp. 68+.

O'Roark, Mary Ann, "The Alarming Rise in Teenage Suicide," *McCalls*, 109, January, 1982, pp. 12-14.

STAGE FOUR: PUBLISHING

Here is the order you should use in submitting your final copy:

1. Title Page.
2. Outline, if required.
3. The final "typed" copy.
4. Endnotes page.
5. Bibliography page.
6. Enclose your report in a clear cover--Make your report look good!**

Your final copy could be bound in a neat hard plastic folder. It could be used in your library's reference section for future "researcher."

The Adventures of Huckleberry Finn is a story of a marvelous boy. Written in authentic colloquial style, it contains adventure, comedy, myth, and unforgettable characters. Above all it is the story of Huck's moral growth.

Early on Huck begins to identify the evils in his society, and he seeks to escape them by the river, the world of truth. He and Jim live according to their own standards. Enter the Duke and the Dolphin, and the problem of evil again confronts them. Huck learns coping skills, the ability to analyze man's faults, and uses them for Jim's and his survival.

Huck's sense of responsibility heightens. He worries about the right and the wrong of his own acts. He witnesses the hypocrisy and the heartlessness of man but does not become a cynic. He grows in compassion. Nurtured by Jim's influence, Huck's moral code grows. In Jim's world, Huck discovers the unshakable values he never finds on shore. Difficult moral decisions become habitual, and impossible heroism becomes achievable.

PREVIEWING EXERCISE

Read these questions before you read the novel and answer as you go along.

1. **What** are some of the social evils Huck identifies?
2. **What** is his initial personal solution for these evils?
3. **Necessity** brings Huck back in contact with social evils.
   a. What are these?
   b. What compromises does Huck make to cope with these evils?
   c. Give incidents of Huck's lying, cheating, and stealing.
   d. Why does he do these things?
4. **Is** Huck a hypocrite? If not, why? If yes, why?
5. **List** some of the events which disgust and depress Huck. Explain.
6. **Do** these events make Huck a cynic? Why? Why not?
7. **How** so you know Huck has true compassion even for those who perpetrate evil?
8. **What** are some of the positive moral decisions Huck makes?
9. **What** are Huck's true feelings about:
   a. Slavery?
   b. Organized religion?
   c. Cruelty to one's fellow?

Citation (Think) Sheet

Fill out the **Citation Sheet** as you are reading the novel and are discussing it with your teacher.

1. Social evils Huck identifies   Solutions

_____

_____

_____

_____

_____

2. Coping skills Huck learns   How and why he
                                                    used them

_____

_____

_____

_____

3. Events which disgusted and   Proofs of his growing
        depressed Huck   understanding of and
                                                    compassion for
                                                    mankind

_____

_____

_____

_____

_____

4. Heroic actions taken by Huck   Circumstances

_____

_____

_____

_____

_____

_____

Writing Prompt and Controlling Idea

In a multi-paragraph paper, you will analyze and trace the moral maturation of Huck Finn. Because of the many possibilities of this subject, you should be very selective. Divide your paper into several short term goals. Use your **Citation Sheet** as a means of establishing these goals.

Do not try to exhaust all the possibilities but center in on only those aspects which best suit your purpose. One developed example is better than five sketchy ones, so do not try to list every event which disgusted Huck. Pick one (possibly two) which will help you prove that despite his disgust, Huck did not become cynical but grew in understanding and compassion for his fellow man.

You probably will use all or most of the divisions listed on your citation sheet, so again be selective in what you include in your paper.

Organization

The raft trip down the Mississippi gives us a basis for drawing a physical map of Huck's and Jim's journey. Likewise, the moral trip, beginning with Huck's identification of evil up to the point where he is capable of acting heroically, gives us the basis for mapping Huck's maturation. However, his moral development does not take place in a tidy chronological sequence of events. Many of the divisions of your citation sheet will overlap chronologically. You should skillfully and selectively choose aspects from each division which best help you map Huck's moral growth.

Gluing Together Ideas

Each of your developmental paragraphs must be linked with the preceding paragraph. This can be accomplished by the repetition of the key word in your paper, in this case maturation, or by using transitional words that indicate a shift of ideas.

Introductory and Concluding Paragraphs

Using the first division of your **Citation Sheet**, you might write a background information introduction, showing how Huck's moral development began with his disillusionment with society which forced him to seek a solution for it.

The next three divisions could well give concrete illustrations of Huck's grappling with evil and his moral growth as the battle continued.

Your concluding paragraph can present a sense of finality to your paper if it is to be a statement of the moral code which Huck had developed by the time he head out from the territory.

Remember the specific models of introductory and concluding paragraphs are included throughout *Fan the Deck*.

Authors often express ethical values through the ways in which their characters react to problems. In *The Glass Menagerie* the characters are certainly exaggerated examples, but their problems and frustrations are the same as those found in any family unit of any age or place.

Each of the characters has a private world into which he/she sometimes retreats when the real world becomes unbearable. Identification of the problems that the characters face and their means of escaping from those problems can lead to a better understanding of the play.

PREVIEWING QUESTIONS

Read the following questions before you attempt to read *The Glass Menagerie*. They will give you specific details to look for and help you to fill out the citation sheet. Answer the questions as you read the play.

1. What special conditions exist in the Wingfield family that make it an especially difficult situation for the characters?
2. How is the fact that there is tension in the family revealed in the first part of the play?
3. a. What do you learn about Amanda's past in the first scene?
   b. How does she view her past?
   c. What indications are there that her past was not exactly as she remembers it?
4. What do we learn about Laura in scene 2?
5. a. In what ways does it appear that Amanda has been trying to help Laura?
   b. Why have her efforts failed?
   c. What alternative does Amanda decide upon at the end of scene 2?
   d. How does Amanda go about implementing the plan she has formed?
6. Explain how Laura feels and why she reacts as she does at each of the following points:
   a. Her mother tells her to let Jim in.
   b. She starts to join Jim and the family for dinner.
   c. Jim joins Laura in the parlor.
   d. Jim dances with her and kisses her.
   e. Jim explains that he is engaged.
7. What is Amanda's reaction to the failure of her plan?
8. Explain how Jim's visit to the Wingfield home brings about a situation that is threatening and/or trying to a.) Tom b.) Laura c.) Amanda.

Name _____ Period_____

Citation (Think) Sheet

Jot down ideas from your responses to the Previewing Questions about each character's situation.

	Problem Character Faces	Ways Character Reacts to Problems (Methods of Escape)
Tom		
Amanda		
Laura		

SUBJECT

In a multi-paragraph paper, discuss the idea that each of the characters in *The Glass Menagerie* has a private world into which he/she sometimes retreats when the real world becomes unbearable. You will describe the kinds of problems that Tom, Laura, and Amanda have and the ways that they escape from those problems. Your divisions will include an introductory paragraph, developmental paragraphs, and a concluding paragraph.

ORGANIZATION

Since this is a multi-paragraph development, each developmental paragraph should discuss the problems and the means of escape of one of the major characters. As you can see, your paper's content has already been decided for you.

Each paragraph in the body of your paper must have its own controlling idea, method of organization, transition words, and ending. Each should give a detailed, descriptive account of the difficulties that the character faces and the way that he/she copes with these difficulties. Use details to support your statements. The comments on your citation sheet should include the specific ideas to incorporate in each paragraph.

GLUING IDEAS TOGETHER

Each of the developmental paragraphs must be linked with the other paragraphs as well as with the introduction and the conclusion. Each paragraph must relate to the thesis of the paper. The linking of developmental paragraphs can be accomplished by the repetition of the key words in your paper, in this case *problems*, *escape*, or suitable replacements.

INTRODUCTORY AND CONCLUDING PARAGRAPHS

You must include both an introductory and a concluding paragraph for this paper. Your introduction should capture the reader's interest, introduce your topic, and set the tone for your paper. In your introduction, state some background information, (the author and title of the play), give a brief plot summary, and reveal your controlling idea.

Your concluding paragraph should tie your ideas together and give your paper a tone of finality. You might end by summarizing and evaluating the ideas discussed. Use appropriate transition words to indicate the completion of your paper.

CORRECTION SYMBOLS
FOR REVISING AND PROOFREADING

abr................................ abbreviation needed or abused

awk................................ awkward sentence structure

beginning...................... need a *catchy* opening

cap................................ capitalization

combine .... **combine** sentences for variety

dm or **mm** .... dangling or misplaced modifier

ending .... need a *pizazz* ending; not *The End*

expand .... **expand** using journalistic questions

focus............................. no clear main idea

frag............................... sentence fragment

gap .... a word is missing

^ .... insert a word

log................................ not logical

org................................ no organization; need a plan

⊄ .... new paragraph needed

punc .... punctuation

?................................... confusing

rearrange...................... **rearrange** sentence parts

ref................................. reference unclear

rep .... repetition; **subtract**

ro.................................. run-on sentence

seq .... ideas out of order; sequence properly

sp.................................. spelling

spec .... not specific enough; **expand**

subtract .... **subtract** the yuk

trans............................. jumbled ideas; need a transition

var .... vary your sentences; **combine**
and **rearrange**

vp .... verb power

vt .... verb tense inconsistency

wc .... word choice

yuk .... too wordy; **subtract**

TERMINOLOGY

APPOSITIVE
A phrase that explains or means the same as the noun.

> Dr. Zuanella, *the economist at the White House,* (appositive) predicted increased unemployment.

BOYS FAN
A list of connectors used to glue equal ideas--**b**ut **o**r **y**et **s**o **f**or **a**nd **n**or

CHECKLIST SHEET
A list of questions to help students critique a composition in the rewriting stage of the writing process.

CITATION SHEET
Similar to a **Think Sheet**, a Citation Sheet is a specific guide to *cite* examples from a literary work to answer a question. This enables the student-writer to focus on a specific topic for a literary analysis paper.

COMBINING
A sentence skill that joins one sentence with another while maintaining the key ideas but eliminating excess words--a **writer's vocabulary** word. Combining sentences enables the writer to create a variety of sentence structures.

COORDINATING CONJUNCTIONS
Also called connectors in **The Stack the Deck Writing System**, these words glue a word to a word, phrase to phrase, clause to a clause, etc. Here is a list of coordinating conjunctions (connectors):

> but   or   yet   so   for   and   nor

An easy way to remember connectors is to think of the expression **boys fan**.

COMMAND FORM OF THE VERB
The pronoun *you* is often understood in the sentence.

> Please share your story with the class. (*You* understood.)

This is also called second person point of view.

CONTROLLING IDEA
It is one sentence that tells the reader the topic of the paragraph and the writer's opinion about the topic. A controlling idea consists of a topic and key words.

CONVENTION
Correct grammatical form.

ESSAY

A multi-paragraph composition that focuses on one specific topic.

EXPANDING

A **writer's vocabulary** word. Using journalistic questions, the writer can add details and color to sentences. Expanding your ideas with journalistic questions helps to support the main idea in a paragraph. Here is the list of journalistic questions:

who   what   when   where   why   how

FIRST PERSON POINT OF VIEW

A point of view for the way a story or narrative is told. When first person point of view is used, the story-teller is directly involved in the narrative. Here is a list of first person pronouns.

I   we   us   our   my   me   mine

FOCUS

A clear direction for your paper. Sticking to the main idea throughout the paper.

FRAGMENT

A sentence fragment is an incomplete thought. Something is missing. To be complete, a sentence must have a subject and a predicate.

Special Tips to Identify Fragments

A good way to identify fragments is to read your composition *backwards* one sentence at a time. You begin with your last sentence and stop. Does it make sense? This reading *aloud* helps you hear incomplete thoughts.

Jessica stayed in the cabin. Because the temperature outside was freezing.

Because the temperature outside was freezing is a fragment. By reading forward, you might **not** hear the fragment. Your mind automatically **combined** the two sentences. However, by reading one sentence at a time *backwards* and pausing after each sentence, you hear the fragment.

Because the temperature outside was freezing.

If you still cannot tell if your sentence makes sense, read the words **I Believe That** before the sentence you are checking. If the sentence sounds okay, it is probably a complete thought. If the sentence sounds confusing, it is probably a fragment.

I Believe That because the temperature outside was freezing.

Can you hear the fragment?

GAPS

Words or ideas that are missing in a sentence. Sometimes writers write so quickly that they inadvertently skip words. Unfortunately, however, when they reread their writing, they automatically include these *missing* words without realizing this.

GLUE WORD

Traditionally called subordinating conjunctions, glue words connect or show the relationship between clauses which are not equally important.

Alex did not finish his dinner **because** he felt ill.

Glue Words--Subordinating Conjunctions

after	because	since	whenever
although	before	so that	where
as	even though	though	wherever
as if	if	unless	while
as long as	in order that	until	
as though	in order to		

GERUND

A verb-noun ending in *ing*.

Smoking is not allowed in our office.

OBJECTIVE

A goal that needs to be accomplished.

ORGANIZATION

A logical way to arrange ideas in a paragraph.

PARAGRAPH

A group of sentences centering on one specific topic.

PAST TENSE

Memory tense. The action has been completed.

Felipe *fried* the beef in peanut oil.

PREDICATE

The verb or verb phrase in a sentence.

PREPOSITION

A word that shows a relationship between two other words; it indicates location. Also called locators in **The Stack the Deck Writing System**.

Locator Words--Prepositions				
above	below	from	on	toward
across	beneath	in	onto	under
against	beside	inside	out	underneath
along	between	into	outside	up
among	beyond	near	over	with
around	by	nearby	through	
at	down	of	to	
behind				

PRESENT TENSE

The *now* tense of a verb in a sentence; actions taking place while an incident is being observed.

> Ben *slides* down the banister into his grandma's arms.

PROCESS

A paper that explains how to do something or how something is done.

REARRANGING

Moving words around in a sentence to vary the sentence structure and/or emphasize a particular idea for the reader--a **writer's vocabulary** word.

RELATIVE PRONOUNS

Called WH words in **The Stack the Deck Writing System**, these words *relate* one part of a sentence to a word in another part of the sentence. They are called WH words because they begin with WH, except for the word **that**.

> who   whose   which   whom   that
>
> Ginger, *who* works at Hackney's Restaurant in her spare time, was hired by Mulcahy, Pauritsch, and Salvador Accounting Firm.

RUN-ON

A sentence that rambles on and on without proper punctuation. See page 30 for rules for identifying and correcting run-on sentences.

SENTENCE

A group of words that expresses a complete thought.

SENTENCE AMBIGUITY
An unclear sentence that has more than one meaning. Ambiguity causes confusion for the reader.

I saw the Statue of Liberty on the bus this morning.

SUBTRACTING
Eliminating unnecessary words or ideas that do not contribute meaning to a sentence. These unnecessary words or ideas just fill in space. Subtracting is another **writer's vocabulary** word.

STUDENT OBJECTIVES AND EVALUATION SHEET (SOES)
A grading sheet for a writing assignment. It lists the objectives that are to be met. The objectives are similar to the ones listed for the **student learning objectives** at the beginning of the prewriting stage.

SUPPORT
Supplying specific details to elaborate or explain a particular idea.

THINK SHEET
A series of questions to help the writer develop his topic before he begins to write the first draft.

THIRD PERSON POINT OF VIEW
A point of view in which the story-teller is not involved in the story. Here is a list of third person singular and plural personal pronouns:

he she it his her hers they their them

TOPIC
What the paragraph is about--subject.

TRANSITIONAL WORDS
Words used to properly connect ideas in a paragraph or link ideas between paragraphs.

VERB
A word that shows action or state of being. If you have a difficult time identifying verbs, write the phrase *He* or *She*___ above the verb column on the **Sentence Opening Sheet**. Any time you list a word in the verb column, read it with *He*___. If it makes sense, it is probably the verb in the sentence.

Examples: He <u>running</u>.   **no verb**

                    He <u>is</u> <u>running</u>.   **verb**